Fun for Friends

Movie/TV

Trivia

Questions, answers & facts
to challenge your mind!

WS Publishing Group
www.WSPublishingGroup.com
San Diego, California

Movie/TV Trivia

By Alex A. Lluch

Published by WS Publishing Group
San Diego, California
Copyright © 2013 by WS Publishing Group

For inquiries:
Log on to www.WSPublishingGroup.com
Email info@WSPublishingGroup.com

ISBN-13: 978-1-61351-035-3

Printed in China.

Movie/TV Trivia

Congratulations! You've taken the first step to hours of fun – alone, or with your friends – answering the most fun and fascinating trivia questions about Movies and TV shows. Whether you're a fan of epic feature films or only watch cartoon network, this book is for you!

This entertaining book includes hundreds of questions based on common movie and TV knowledge, making it easy for most people to know the answers. However, it also includes details of the film industry's greatest productions that will challenge any movie buff. The best thing about this book: Every question includes highly compelling facts guaranteed to keep you reading for hours.

This book is the perfect companion for road trips, waiting in the DMV line, riding on the subway, or just hanging out at home. Keep this book on hand at work (for those much-needed breaks), in the bedroom (much better than watching reruns), in the bathroom (you might as well do something useful), in the kitchen (while waiting for the water to boil) or anywhere you find yourself with a few minutes to spare. You can even bring it on a first date to fill those awkward silences and keep the conversation flowing.

See an attractive person across the room but don't know how to approach him/her? Initiate the conversation with one of our captivating movie questions like: Which *Apollo 13* astronaut declares, "Houston, we have a problem"? You will feel more confident with your new and improved knowledge, and everyone around you will want to get to know you better.

Friday night blues? Don't know what to do? Invite all your friends over and take turns picking categories and asking each other questions. Make it interesting by proposing fun rules such as: loser pays for drinks, winner gets a back massage, or anything else you can think of!

When you finish this book you will feel smarter, more informed … and maybe even thinner and taller. You'll be ready to test your new movie & TV trivia knowledge against your peers and show them how smart you are. You'll surely be the life of any party, as you'll never run out of interesting topics that make for good conversation.

So whether you're passionate about film or just have a passing interest, you will enjoy learning about movies and TV in this friendly, fun and fact-filled book.

1. Whose song was playing when John Travolta and Uma Thurman did the "Twist" in *Pulp Fiction*?

a) Al Green
b) Dusty Springfield
c) Chuck Berry
d) Urge Overkill

2. What was the minimum *Speed* Sandra Bullock had to maintain while driving the bus?

a) 65 mph
b) 60 mph
c) 45 mph
d) 50 mph

3. In *National Treasure* Nicholas Cage plays a character named after which Founding Father?

a) George Washington
b) Benjamin Franklin
c) Thomas Jefferson
d) John Adams

4. In the *Kill Bill* films, Uma Thurman's revenge-seeking character is identified as who?

a) "Death's Yellow Lady"
b) "The Killer"
c) "The Woman"
d) "The Bride"

5. Whip-wielding archaeologist *Indiana Jones* is identified with which kind of hat?

a) fedora
b) cowboy hat
c) safari hat
d) Panama hat

Action & Thriller

Answers

1. Chuck Berry

"You Never Can Tell" wailed as Travolta crafted – what many believed to be – a dark update to his 1977 *Saturday Night Fever* character.

2. 50 mph

The budget was depleted before filming finished. The first test audiences were shown storyboards of the unfilmed scenes.

3. Benjamin Franklin

His dad was named after a Founder (Patrick Henry), and so was every Gates family member identified in the film.

4. "The Bride"

Inspired by their conversation while filming *Pulp Fiction*, Tarantino gave Thurman the movie as a 30th birthday present.

5. fedora

The bullwhip scar on Indy's chin was actually a real-life scar that Ford received from a car accident when he was 20.

1. In 2012 Meryl Streep won her third Academy Award for playing which *Iron Lady*?

a) Queen Elizabeth II
b) Sister Aloysius Beauvier
c) Julia Child
d) Margaret Thatcher

2. In 1998 Judi Dench and Cate Blanchett were both Oscar nominees for playing which queen?

a) Queen Elizabeth I
b) Queen Elizabeth II
c) Queen Victoria
d) Marie Antoinette

3. Phillip Seymour Hoffman's *Capote* chronicled the author as he worked on which book?

a) *Breakfast at Tiffany's*
b) *The Grass Harp*
c) *In Cold Blood*
d) *Answered Prayers*

4. *Good Night and Good Luck* detailed Edward R. Murrow's journalistic crusade against whom?

a) Joseph McCarthy
b) Eugene McCarthy
c) communists
d) Richard Nixon

5. Which *Apollo 13* astronaut declares, "Houston, we have a problem."?

a) Gordon Cooper
b) Jack Swigert
c) Alan Shepard
d) Jim Lovell

Biography
Answers

1. Margaret Thatcher

She has received many Oscar nods for playing real people: Julia Child, Susan Orlean, Karen Blixsen and Karen Silkwood.

2. Queen Elizabeth I

They starred together in the '06 drama, *Notes on a Scandal*, for which Dench received a nomination for Best Actress and Blanchett, Best Supporting.

3. *In Cold Blood*

Despite his diminutive size (5'3"), Capote was reputed to be a formidable arm wrestler. He was also a Studio 54 regular.

4. Joseph McCarthy

Test audiences thought that the man who played McCarthy overacted, but it was actually archival film of the real person.

5. Jim Lovell

It was one of the only unfaithful scenes in the film – Swigert was actually the first to utter "Houston, *we've had* a problem."

1. A Sharpie was used to add the spots on "Dalmatian mice" in what Wes Anderson film?

   a) *Rushmore*
   b) *The Darjeeling Limited*
   c) *The Royal Tenenbaums*
   d) *Moonrise Kingdom*

2. What compels the two male leads to go on the run disguised as women in *Some Like It Hot*?

   a) They witness a mob hit.
   b) They stole some money.
   c) They killed someone.
   d) They broke out of prison.

3. Which eventual star was only seen as a corpse after his part was cut from *The Big Chill*?

   a) Richard Gere
   b) Kevin Costner
   c) Tom Hanks
   d) Mel Gibson

4. The two dolts in *Dumb & Dumber* drove cross-country in a van outfitted to look like what?

   a) a cheetah
   b) an airplane
   c) a dog
   d) a house

5. In *The Graduate* Ben Braddock is advised by his parents' friend to go into what job field?

   a) accounting
   b) food service
   c) paid escorting
   d) plastics

1. *The Royal Tenenbaums*

   The hawk that "played" Richie's pet Mordecai was kidnapped during filming and held for ransom, leading to its recasting.

2. **They witness a mob hit.**

   The film was banned from showing in Kansas because state legislators felt cross-dressing was "too disturbing."

3. **Kevin Costner**

   To make it up to him, director Lawrence Kasdan promised Costner a principal role in his following film, *Silverado*.

4. **a dog**

   Carrey, whose front tooth was really chipped, ad-libbed many of the film's best moments including "the most annoying sound in the world."

5. **plastics**

   He may not have heeded the advice, but others did – the plastic industry boomed in the year following the film's release.

1. In *The Godfather* a Corleone hitman cleans up a murder by leaving the gun but taking what?

   a) a cannoli
   b) a horse's head
   c) a car
   d) money

2. Which movie introduced filmgoers to the literary characters Atticus, Scout and Boo?

   a) *Grapes of Wrath*
   b) *E.T.*
   c) *To Kill a Mockingbird*
   d) *High Noon*

3. Which James Dean movie was the star's only film to be released before his sudden death?

   a) *Rebel Without a Cause*
   b) *East of Eden*
   c) *Giant*
   d) none of these

4. What or who was the title character's "Rosebud" in Orson Welles' *Citizen Kane*?

   a) his mother
   b) the first woman he loved
   c) his boyhood sled
   d) his boyhood dog

5. Which TV creator and writer is known for his "walking and talking" scenes?

   a) Matthew Weiner
   b) Aaron Sorkin
   c) Steven Bochco
   d) David Chase

1. *a cannoli*

The Corleones may have demanded devotion, but the film's star didn't; Marlon Brando read all of his lines off cue cards.

2. *To Kill a Mockingbird*

In 2003, the American Film Institute listed Gregory Peck's Atticus Finch as the greatest cinematic hero of all time.

3. *East of Eden*

The troubled, red-jacketed Rebel made him an icon and both post-mortem releases earned him Oscar nominations.

4. **his boyhood sled**

Kane could buy anything except for love. His last word was the name of the only thing that ever brought him true joy.

5. **Aaron Sorkin**

Sorkin has previously worked as a "script doctor," remedying scripts like *The Rock*, *Enemy of the State* and *Bulworth*.

1. Which college was the alma mater of *The Cosby's Show*'s Cliff and Clair Huxtable?

   a) Spelman
   b) Princeton
   c) Howard
   d) Hillman

2. What name do Woody and Buzz have written on the soles of their feet?

   a) Walt
   b) Andy
   c) Tommy
   d) Sam

3. Halloween classic *Hocus Pocus* was set in what storied city?

   a) Greenwich, CT
   b) Boston, MA
   c) Philadelphia, PA
   d) Salem, MA

4. Which food did Snoopy **not** serve when he fixed Thanksgiving dinner for the Peanuts Gang?

   a) jellybeans
   b) waffles
   c) buttered toast
   d) pretzels

5. Charlie Brown longs to receive a Valentine from which classmate?

   a) Lucy Van Pelt
   b) Frieda, with the curly hair
   c) the Little Red-Haired Girl
   d) the Pretty Blue-Eyed Girl

1. Hillman

The fictional Hillman was the setting for the show's spin-off, *A Different World*, which followed Denise to college.

2. Andy

Toy Story is one of only two animations on AFI's list of greats. Pixar wanted Jim Carrey and Paul Newman for the roles but couldn't afford them.

3. Salem, MA

When a virgin lit a candle, three witches were brought back to life in modern Salem, 300 years after their hanging.

4. waffles

Once the gang leaves, Snoopy and Woodstock shared the traditional turkey dinner that the kids didn't think he could cook.

5. the Little Red-Haired Girl

"I like you Charlie Brown," said the note she gave him on the last day of school, to the delight of his lovesick heart.

1. Half of Norman Bates psyche belonged to himself and the other belonged to whom?

   a) his dead mother
   b) the devil
   c) his dead twin brother
   d) a fictional murderer

2. In which classic fright film does a character lament, "We're gonna need a bigger boat."?

   a) *The Shining*
   b) *Alien*
   c) *Jaws*
   d) *The Poseidon Adventure*

3. In which film was the danger preceded by a little girl's ominous report: "They're here!"?

   a) *Poltergeist*
   b) *The Omen*
   c) *The Sixth Sense*
   d) *The Exorcist*

4. Richard Dreyfuss molds Devil's Tower with what food in *Close Encounters of the Third Kind*?

   a) fruit
   b) ice cream
   c) oatmeal
   d) mashed potatoes

5. In a discussion with Clarice Starling, Hannibal Lecter describes a meal featuring what?

   a) filet mignon and a Bordeaux
   b) fava beans and Chianti
   c) saffron risotto and Champagne
   d) tea biscuits and Earl Grey

1. his dead mother

Hitchcock shot *Psycho* in black and white because he felt it would be too gory in color. It was his final black and white film.

2. *Jaws*

The film's animatronic shark was broken for much of the shoot, which is why it remained unseen until late in the movie.

3. *Poltergeist*

Drew Barrymore auditioned for the girl's role but didn't get it. However, it *did* land her the star-making role in Spielberg's *E.T.*

4. mashed potatoes

The theme from Stephen Spielberg's *Jaws* can be heard when the alien ship communicates. Dreyfuss was also in *Jaws*.

5. fava beans and Chianti

The American Film Institute listed Starling as one of cinema's greatest heroes and Lecter as the top villain.

Reality TV & Talk Show
Questions

1. How many strangers lived together – starting the reality TV fad – in *The Real World*'s debut?

 a) five
 b) six
 c) seven
 d) eight

2. Long-tagged the series' best player, who finally won "Sole Survivor" on their fourth try?

 a) Russell Hantz
 b) Richard Hatch
 c) "Boston" Rob Mariano
 d) Benjamin "Coach" Wade

3. What does the hand gesture Donald Trump delivers with his *Apprentice* catchphrase resemble?

 a) karate chop
 b) serpent strike
 c) scissors cutting
 d) backhanded slap

4. Which American womenswear designer is a regular judge on Project Runway?

 a) Ralph Lauren
 b) Michael Kors
 c) Tim Gunn
 d) Isaac Mizrahi

5. What are Top Chef contestants asked to pack when they are eliminated from competition?

 a) their knives
 b) their tools
 c) their utensils
 d) their dishes

1. **seven**

It also launched the debate about reality TV content, after social themes in the early seasons gave way to wild antics.

2. **"Boston" Rob Mariano**

At the end of his second attempt, prior to being named runner-up, he proposed to future Survivor winner, Amber Brkich.

3. **serpent strike**

Show contestants actually stay in a penthouse on the same level as the boardroom, so they don't take an elevator up (like Trump tells them to).

4. **Michael Kors**

Famous show catchphrases include mentor Gunn's, "Make it work" and the second season's joke, "What happened to Andre?"

5. **their knives**

The show has introduced concepts like molecular gastronomy and the versatility of foam to mainstream foodies.

1. Where did *Casablanca's* Rick and Ilsa engage in their doomed affair before meeting again in Casablanca?

   a) New York City
   b) Paris
   c) London
   d) Berlin

2. How many directors led the production of *Gone with the Wind*?

   a) zero
   b) two
   c) three
   d) four

3. What were the rival gangs in *West Side Story*?

   a) Pink Ladies and T-Birds
   b) Snakes and Sharks
   c) Jets and Lions
   d) Jets and Sharks

4. The meeting that never took place in *An Affair to Remember* was to occur at what location?

   a) Eiffel Tower
   b) Empire State Building
   c) Statue of Liberty
   d) Big Ben

5. Where was Sally when she made her "climactic" demonstration for Harry?

   a) airport
   b) church
   c) movie theater
   d) deli

1. Paris

Many of the film's Nazis were played by
Jews who had fled from Nazi Germany.
The director Michael Curtiz and the three
screenwriters were also Jewish.

2. three

Producer David O. Selznick also asked
Alfred Hitchcock to script a scene, but none
of his treatment was ever filmed.

3. Jets and Sharks

The director encouraged the rival gang
actors to play pranks on one another
to maintain real tension between the
two groups.

4. Empire State Building

While it was only AFI's fifth best romantic
movie, it's their highest-ranking film in
which the couple is together in the end.

5. deli

Her performance prompted a nearby diner
– played by the director's mother – to tell a
waiter, "I'll have what she's having."

1. Where does Amélie find the box that sparks her spirited adventure of generous deeds?

   a) under a floorboard
   b) behind an exposed brick
   c) behind a bathroom tile
   d) in the ceiling

2. Among the most celebrated films of the 2000s was this underworld fairytale set in fascist Spain.

   a) *Volver*
   b) *Pan's Labyrinth*
   c) *Biutiful*
   d) *The Crime of Father Amaro*

3. Before acting, the Wicked Witch of the West, Margaret Hamilton, was employed as a:

   a) flight attendant
   b) kindergarten teacher
   c) model
   d) monkey trainer

4. Which show's tropical polar bears and unseen "Smoke Monster" perplexed viewers?

   a) *Lost*
   b) *The X-Files*
   c) *Once Upon a Time*
   d) *Revolution*

5. How did Dr. Sam Beckett try to "put right what once went wrong"?

   a) by solving crimes
   b) by acting as ghost's medium
   c) by solving medical mysteries
   d) by leaping through time

1. behind a bathroom tile

The American Society of Cinematographers selected *Amélie*, set in an idealized Paris, as the best shot film of the 2000s.

2. *Pan's Labyrinth*

Director Guillermo del Toro based the film's myriad details on sketches he had been making in notebooks for 20 years.

3. kindergarten teacher

During a take, her copper-based make-up accidentally caught on fire. Her frightening performance was cut from the film.

4. *Lost*

The crashed plane used for the set was a Lochheed Tristar priced at $200,000. It was dismantled in Mojave and shipped to Hawaii in pieces.

5. by leaping through time

"Project Quantum Leap" sent Sam careening through the past; TV Guide rated it one of the top cult shows of all-time.

1. Which foreign director made a memorable spectacle when he climbed on seats at the Oscars?

a) Roberto Benigni
b) Pedro Almodóvar
c) Guillermo del Toro
d) Ang Lee

2. Which war movie ends with the image of a hand reaching for a butterfly?

a) *The Bridge on the River Kwai*
b) *All Quiet on the Western Front*
c) *The Great Escape*
d) *Sergeant York*

3. Which *Apocalypse Now* actor said the line, "I love the smell of napalm in the morning"?

a) Martin Sheen
b) Marlon Brando
c) Dennis Hopper
d) Robert Duvall

4. What did Robert Redford's *Sundance Kid* admit as he teetered on the edge of a cliff?

a) He was afraid of heights.
b) He couldn't swim.
c) Butch was his best friend.
d) He didn't want to die.

5. John Wayne and Jeff Bridges have both played which cinematic Old West hero?

a) Davy Crockett
b) Rooster Cogburn
c) Ethan Edwards
d) Jesse James

1. Roberto Benigni

Life Is Beautiful's award was presented by fellow Italian Sophia Loren, who Benigni said he wanted even more than Oscar.

2. *All Quiet on the Western Front*

The iconic scene was added during editing. With the actors unavailable, the director filmed his own hand instead.

3. Robert Duvall

During production Typhoon Olga wrecked the sets, Sheen suffered a heart attack and Coppola dropped 100 pounds.

4. He couldn't swim.

The scene's jump was filmed on location in Colorado; the water landing was filmed in a studio lake in California.

5. Rooster Cogburn

Wayne won an Oscar for his *True Grit* performance. Bridges was likely happy to settle for a nomination for his turn in the role.

1. In which city did Rocky triumphantly run up a flight of stone steps?

a) New York City
b) Philadelphia
c) Chicago
d) Boston

2. Which thriller's seasons all began at a very specific time of day, usually in the morning?

a) *Alias*
b) *Prison Break*
c) *24*
d) *Mission: Impossible*

3. What real-life brothers dropped out of the roles of Virgil and Turk Malloy in *Ocean's 11*?

a) Mark & Donnie Wahlberg
b) Alec & William Baldwin
c) Ben & Casey Affleck
d) Owen & Luke Wilson

4. What big-screen big leaguer bought Buckner's '86 World Series booted ball for $93,000?

a) Kevin Costner
b) Robert Redford
c) Charlie Sheen
d) Tim Robbins

5. Which movie holds the record for most Academy Award nominations earned by a foreign film?

a) *Amélie*
b) *Crouching Tiger, Hidden Dragon*
c) *Life Is Beautiful*
d) *Like Water for Chocolate*

1. Philadelphia

During the film's famous jogging scene, Stallone injured his leg and had to be taken to the hospital in a wheelbarrow.

2. *24*

The show actually added three minutes to the clock throughout each episode to leave time for previews and commercials.

3. Owen & Luke Wilson

The Wilsons dropped out to make *The Royal Tenenbaums* instead, as did Danny Glover, who was going to play Frank.

4. Charlie Sheen

Star of *Eight Men Out* and *Major League*, Sheen sold the ball in 2000 for $63,500. His buyer sold it in 2012 for $418,250.

5. *Crouching Tiger, Hidden Dragon*

The ten-time nominee was also the first martial arts movie to get a nod, and is the top-grossing foreign film of all time.

1. Which actor played the first American in space in *The Right Stuff*?

a) Ed Harris
b) Scott Glenn
c) Dennis Quaid
d) Sam Shepard

2. *The Diving Bell and the Butterfly* is about a man with which rare neurological condition?

a) Bell's palsy
b) encephalitis
c) meningitis
d) locked-in syndrome

3. How many actors portrayed incarnations of Bob Dylan in the biopic, *I'm Not There.*?

a) two actors
b) three actors
c) four actors
d) six actors

4. In *The Last King of Scotland* Forest Whitaker played Idi Amin, a president of which country?

a) Scotland
b) Rwanda
c) Uganda
d) Somalia

5. Michael Sheen played David Frost in a film about his exchanges with which historic figure?

a) Richard Nixon
b) Harvey Milk
c) Marilyn Monroe
d) Princess Diana

Biography

Answers

1. Scott Glenn

Alan Shepard wrote to the director praising the portrayal of him but noted Glenn's failure to be as handsome as he was.

2. locked-in syndrome

Based on Jean-Dominique Bauby's memoir, he communicated the book to a transcriber solely by blinking. The book took 200,000 blinks to write.

3. six actors

As of 2008, Cate Blanchett had five Oscar nods and four of those roles (including Dylan) were for playing real people.

4. Uganda

Amin's real-life self-bestowed title included, "Lord of All the Beasts of the Earth and Fishes of the Seas."

5. Richard Nixon

To maintain friction, the *Frost/Nixon* cast remained in character even off-camera, teasing each other and feigning arguments.

1. What was the name of the Manhattan diner patronized by Jerry, Elaine, George and Kramer?

a) Al's
b) Joe's
c) Monk's
d) The Diner

2. To test whether a lifeless "Ugly Naked Guy" was dead, the *Friends* made a poking device out of:

a) wire hangers
b) chopsticks
c) plastic utensils
d) pencils

3. On *The Big Bang Theory*, according to Sheldon, Penny can only sing "Soft Kitty" when?

a) he's accomplished something
b) he feels sad
c) he needs help falling asleep
d) he's sick

4. What is Phil always forgetting to fix in the Dunphy house on *Modern Family*?

a) a stuck drawer
b) a broken stair
c) the attic ladder
d) the kitchen table

5. Which musical comedy ends with an acquitted duo lighting up the stage with machine guns?

a) *Chicago*
b) *Moulin Rouge*!
c) *Burlesque*
d) *The Rocky Horror Picture Show*

1. Monk's

The fictional eatery was home to the "big salad" and George's attempts to eat candy bars with a knife and fork.

2. chopsticks

Bruce Willis guest starred on *Friends* for free after losing a bet to *Whole Nine Yards'* costar, Matthew Perry. Willis won an Emmy for his appearance.

3. he's sick

Originally named *Lenny, Penny, and Kenny*, only one person on the show has a PhD in real life: regular guest star, Mayim Bialik.

4. a broken stair

After he failed to do it for two seasons, Claire finally tried to fix the step but ripped it off in frustration instead.

5. *Chicago*

The film version had been in the works since the '70s. Back then, Frank Sinatra, Goldie Hawn and Liza Minnelli were the planned stars.

1. Which cop show is tied with *Gunsmoke* as the longest-running primetime drama?

   a) *Hill Street Blues*
   b) *Law & Order*
   c) *NYPD Blue*
   d) *Dragnet*

2. Which star of NBC's medical drama *ER* was previously in a sitcom also titled *E/R*?

   a) Julianna Margulies
   b) Noah Wyle
   c) Anthony Edwards
   d) George Clooney

3. What song was playing right before *The Sopranos'* ambiguous final fade to black?

   a) "Don't Stop Believin'"
   b) "If I Can Dream"
   c) "My Way"
   d) "Born to Run"

4. Which *The West Wing* cast member was not originally a series regular?

   a) Rob Lowe
   b) Martin Sheen
   c) Allison Janney
   d) Bradley Whitford

5. On which Manhattan boulevard is *Mad Men's* Sterling Cooper ad agency located?

   a) Fifth Avenue
   b) Park Avenue
   c) Madison Avenue
   d) Broadway

1. ***Law & Order***

   The 20-season tie is eclipsed by the *Law & Order* franchise's collective run: 46 seasons and counting, as of 2012.

2. **George Clooney**

   He was a TV vet from *Facts of Life*, *Roseanne* and both medical shows before earning film fame and seven Oscar nods.

3. **"Don't Stop Believin'"**

   The rock tune heralded the drama's controversial dark finish in '07 and the start of the dark comedy *Glee* in '09.

4. **Martin Sheen**

   Initially slated for just the pilot, the president was ultimately the show's moral compass, and earned Sheen six Emmy nods.

5. **Madison Avenue**

   Mad Men was the nickname for '60s N.Y. advertising pros, since so many agencies were located on this famous street.

1. Simba's father Mufasa was brought to life in *The Lion King* by this "Voice of CNN":

   a) Morgan Freeman
   b) Walter Cronkite
   c) James Earl Jones
   d) Sean Connery

2. Simba's best friends in *The Lion King*, Timon and Pumbaa, are what kind of animals?

   a) mongoose and warthog
   b) mongoose and boar
   c) meerkat and boar
   d) meerkat and warthog

3. The fairies who raise *Sleeping Beauty* fight over making her dress one of which two colors?

   a) purple or pink
   b) red or blue
   c) pink or blue
   d) red or purple

4. What object symbolizes the time the Beast has remaining to get someone to love him?

   a) hourglass
   b) rose
   c) painting
   d) candle

5. What kind of creatures are Flotsam and Jetsam, Ursula's minions, in *The Little Mermaid*?

   a) octopuses
   b) squids
   c) eels
   d) sea snakes

1. James Earl Jones

When Mufasa tells Simba that the stars represent great kings of the past, a constellation of Mickey Mouse is visible.

2. meerkat and warthog

In nature they are unlikely friends, but warthogs do pal around with striped mongooses, who groom them of ticks.

3. pink or blue

Disney has no record of (nor does the film give a credit to) the actress who provided the voice for Aurora's mother.

4. rose

Much of the characterization for Belle was based on Katharine Hepburn's portrayal of Josephine March in *Little Women*.

5. eels

In Hans Christian Anderson's original story the prince marries someone else and the Little Mermaid dissolves to foam.

1. Stanley Kubrick's *The Shining* was based on a novel by whom?

   a) John Grisham
   b) Michael Crichton
   c) Anne Rice
   d) Stephen King

2. What young actress gained fame for spewing bile as her head spun in *The Exorcist*?

   a) Tatum O'Neal
   b) Linda Blair
   c) Jodie Foster
   d) Drew Barrymore

3. Where did *The Thing* attack Kurt Russell and his fellow researchers?

   a) Norway
   b) Antarctic
   c) Finland
   d) Greenland

4. Which legendary horror villain runs amuck in *Halloween*?

   a) Freddy Krueger
   b) Jason
   c) Michael Myers
   d) Norman Bates

5. Who played the object of Kathy Bates' psychotic fixation in Rob Reiner's *Misery*?

   a) James Caan
   b) Tommy Lee Jones
   c) Ray Liotta
   d) Jack Nicholson

1. Stephen King

The subject matter of *The Shining* prompted Kubrick to call King late at night during filming to ask if he believed in God.

2. Linda Blair

Evangelist, Billy Graham, believed that demons lived in the film's reels. Blair got so many threats, the studio had to get bodyguards.

3. Antarctic

To mimic the sub-zero conditions of the South Pole in 100-degree L.A., the movie sets were refrigerated to 40° F.

4. Michael Myers

Halloween's leading lady, Jamie Lee Curtis, is the daughter of Janet Leigh who starred in Psycho, AFI's greatest horror film of all time.

5. James Caan

Bates was the first Oscar winner for a horror film. Stephen King was so awed that he wrote later novels with her in mind.

1. Where do the titles for episodes of *The Amazing Race* come from?

   a) the name of the destination
   b) a quote in that episode
   c) the name of the challenge
   d) which leg of the race is shown

2. After 24 seasons of *The Bachelor/Bachelorette*, how many final couples have gotten married?

   a) zero
   b) two
   c) four
   d) ten

3. Which comedian survived the elements with Bear Grylls in an episode of *Man vs. Wild*?

   a) Jim Carrey
   b) Stephen Colbert
   c) Will Ferrell
   d) Jon Stewart

4. What prize does the ballroom champion of *Dancing with the Stars* receive?

   a) Dance Floor Diamond Pin
   b) Crystal Ballroom Trophy
   c) Mirror Ball Trophy
   d) Sterling Step Statue

5. Who was the first *American Idol*?

   a) Fantasia Barrino
   b) Ruben Studdard
   c) Justin Guarini
   d) Kelly Clarkson

Reality TV & Talk Show
Answers

1. a quote in that episode

In the first 10 years that an Emmy was awarded in the Reality Competition category, *Amazing Race* won nine times.

2. two

Both marriages were a result of *The Bachelorette*: Trista & Ryan Sutter, and Ashley & JP Rosenbaum. Bachelor Jason Mesnick wed his runner-up.

3. Will Ferrell

Ferrell ate the "Emergency Twinkie" Grylls gave him within seconds of getting it. Later the pair ate a reindeer eyeball.

4. Mirror Ball Trophy

Athletes do well in the ballroom: seven of the show's first 15 winners were jocks. The first athlete to win on the show was Emmitt Smith.

5. Kelly Clarkson

Season 4's Idol Carrie Underwood had the top career though, with five Grammys and 13.5 million albums sold as of 2012.

1. In the opening scene, what was Holly Golightly eating for breakfast in front of Tiffany's?

   a) donut
   b) slice of pizza
   c) hotdog
   d) danish

2. What song was playing when Baby leapt into Johnny's arms in Dirty Dancing?

   a) "Stay"
   b) "The Time of My Life"
   c) "She's Like the Wind"
   d) "What a Feeling"

3. Which Woody Allen romantic comedy was originally intended to be a murder mystery?

   a) *Manhattan*
   b) *Midnight in Paris*
   c) *Annie Hall*
   d) *Mighty Aphrodite*

4. What high school did Danny and Sandy attend in Grease?

   a) Rydell High
   b) Beverly Hills High
   c) Franklin High
   d) Marshall High

5. Which character in The Princess Bride wants to avenge the death of their father?

   a) Westley
   b) Buttercup
   c) Inigo Montoya
   d) Vizzini

1. **danish**

Audrey Hepburn detested danishes and begged to eat a ice cream instead, but the director refused her pleas.

2. **"The Time of My Life"**

The giggling and falling in their scenes as Grey's character learned to dance was genuine, as was Swayze's frustration.

3. *Annie Hall*

Unbeknownst to Allen, the passerby he describes as "the winner of a Truman Capote look-a-like contest" was actually the real Truman Capote.

4. **Rydell High**

The slumber party scene, in which Rizzo sings a song with a lyric about Elvis, was coincidentally filmed the day that Presley died.

5. **Inigo Montoya**

Rob Reiner couldn't be on-set when Billy Crystal filmed his scenes because he would laugh so hard that it made him sick.

1. Benjamin Button, who curiously aged backwards, hailed from what legendary city?

   a) Paris
   b) New York City
   c) New Orleans
   d) Chicago

2. What substance are New Yorkers left wiping off of themselves at the end of *Ghostbusters*?

   a) green slime
   b) marshmallow
   c) proton streamers
   d) black slime

3. What town did George Bailey discover was worse off without him in *It's a Wonderful Life*?

   a) Mount Washington
   b) Springfield
   c) Havenhill
   d) Bedford Falls

4. *Buffy the Vampire Slayer*'s Rupert first gained fame as a spokesman for what coffee brand?

   a) Taster's Choice
   b) Folgers
   c) Maxwell House
   d) Café Britt

5. Approximately 14,000 scripts arrived when viewers were invited to submit ideas for what '60s sci-fi hit?

   a) *Star Trek*
   b) *The Twilight Zone*
   c) *The Jetsons*
   d) *The Outer Limits*

Sci-Fi & Fantasy

Answers

1. New Orleans

He was born the same year that a noted WWI memorial clock that ran backwards was unveiled in the city's train station.

2. marshmallow

They destroyed the Stay Puft Marshmallow Man by blowing it up – its remains were simulated with shaving cream.

3. Bedford Falls

Without George, Bedford Falls became "Pottersville," after it was taken over by the town's bank-owning Scrooge.

4. Taster's Choice

His home in Somerset, England was used for filming several *Buffy* episodes. He auditioned to be (the eighth) *Doctor Who*.

5. *The Twilight Zone*

Robert Redford, Robert Duvall and Dennis Hopper appeared on Rod Serling's show in their early careers.

1. *Dances with Wolves'* success was surprising because much of the dialogue was what language?

   a) Creole
   b) Russian
   c) Lakota
   d) Chinese

2. What did the Allied POWs in *The Great Escape* name their three tunnels?

   a) Mary, Betty & Susie
   b) Jesus, Mary & Joseph
   c) Tubman, Douglass & Lincoln
   d) Tom, Dick & Harry

3. Which Meryl Streep role did *Premiere* rank as the third greatest film performance ever?

   a) Sophie, *Sophie's Choice*
   b) Karen, *Silkwood*
   c) Linda, *The Deer Hunter*
   d) Lindy, *A Cry in the Dark*

4. Which actor made his film debut in the desert epic, *Lawrence of Arabia*?

   a) Anthony Quinn
   b) Alec Guinness
   c) Peter O'Toole
   d) Omar Sharif

5. The 2009 film, *Waltz with Bashir*, was the Academy Award's first Foreign Language Film nominee to be:

   a) directed by a minor
   b) in English
   c) black and white
   d) animated

1. Lakota

The language varies by gender. When Stands With A Fist taught Dunbar how to speak, she taught him to speak like a Lakota woman.

2. Tom, Dick & Harry

Based in part on a true story, the "Tunnel King" who built most of the real Tom, Dick and Harry, advised the film.

3. Sophie Zawistowski, *Sophie's Choice*

She insisted on shooting the final scene in one take and refused to watch it. She saw it for the first time 14 years later on the *Oprah Winfrey Show*.

4. Peter O'Toole

Marking his first role as a title character, *Premiere* Magazine ranked his performance #1 in their list of 100 Greatest Performances of All Time.

5. animated

The film examines the real-life experiences of Israeli movie director/producer Ari Folman in the 1982 Lebanon War. The film was ultimately banned in Lebanon.

1. The sequel to which thriller was teased with "Something Has Survived"?

a) *Dr. No*
b) *Jurassic Park*
c) *The Terminator*
d) *Planet of the Apes*

2. Which criminal organization convinced Sydney Bristow it was part of the CIA on *Alias*?

a) SD-6
b) A.L.I.A.S.
c) Unit 99
d) Q-17

3. What is the high school team's mascot in the first three seasons of *Friday Night Lights*?

a) Ranger
b) Tiger
c) Longhorn
d) Panther

4. What TV show crashed and replaced at least 250 cars during the course of the series?

a) *Miami Vice*
b) *Knight Rider*
c) *The Dukes of Hazzard*
d) *Starsky & Hutch*

5. What man of action died, only to "return" in the flesh for a surprise successive season?

a) Thomas Magnum
b) Jack Bauer
c) Steve Austin
d) Sonny Crockett

1. *Jurassic Park*

A year before Michael Crichton's book was published (or even complete), Universal offered him $2 million for the rights and commenced production.

2. SD-6

All of the first season's narration was recorded via telephone. Jennifer Garner was working on location and had to call her lines in to J.J. Abrams.

3. Panther

FNL initially uses the same mascot as the book and movie that informed it. The show ends featuring the East Dillon Lions.

4. *The Dukes of Hazzard*

Dodge stopped making Chargers in 1978, so producers had to buy them from people on the street.

5. Thomas Magnum

Magnum was killed and spent the intended series finale as a ghost. Fan outcry led to a new season and his resurrection.

1. Which documentary about reclusive Kennedy-in-laws was remade into a movie starring Jessica Lange?

a) *The Really Big Family*
b) *Grey Gardens*
c) *Four Days in November*
d) *Hearts and Minds*

2. *When We Were Kings* detailed the 1974 "Rumble in the Jungle" boxing match between whom?

a) Muhammad Ali & Sonny Listo
b) Muhammad Ali & Joe Frazier
c) Muhammad Ali & Joe Louis
d) Muhammad Ali & George Foreman

3. *The War Room* chronicled the inner-workings of which presidential candidate's campaign?

a) George W. Bush
b) Bill Clinton
c) Ronald Reagan
d) Richard Nixon

4. Which critically acclaimed documentary was originally intended to be a 30-minute PBS special?

a) *The War Room*
b) *The Fog of War*
c) *Hoop Dreams*
d) *Woodstock*

5. Fill in the blank: *Enron: The _____ Guys in the Room.*

a) Greediest
b) Loudest
c) Craziest
d) Smartest

1. *Grey Gardens*

Lange and Drew Barrymore play recluses Edith and little Edie Beale, once enviable socialites who wind up living in flea-infested squalor.

2. *Muhammad Ali & George Foreman*

Using the rope-a-dope technique, Ali reclaimed the boxing title taken from him four years earlier after he refused the Vietnam Draft.

3. Bill Clinton

Shot in Little Rock, the film starred Clinton's "Ragin' Cajun" strategist Carville and former Boy Wonder, Stephanopoulos.

4. *Hoop Dreams*

Few documentaries are as highly praised. Roger Ebert said it's "one of the best films about American life [he's] ever seen."

5. *Smartest*

Condé Nast Portfolio named Ken Lay third worst American CEO ever, 8 spots ahead of Henry Frick, a man so hated he was shot thrice in 1892.

1. Which *Seinfeld* character's dancing was like a "full-body dry heave set to music"?

a) Elaine's
b) Kramer's
c) Jerry's
d) Newman's

2. What talk show-within-a-show opened with: "Live, on tape, from Hollywood..."?

a) *Coffee Talk*
b) *The Hollywood Hour*
c) *The Larry Sanders Show*
d) *The Late Night Show*

3. Which SNL regular is remembered for playing a Chippendale's dancer and speaker Matt Foley?

a) Dana Carvey
b) Chris Farley
c) David Spade
d) Adam Sandler

4. Which game show host played Ferris Bueller's repetitive monotoned teacher?

a) Alex Trebeck
b) Hugh Downs
c) Jack Paar
d) Ben Stein

5. Which comedy was **not** a collaboration between actor Hugh Grant and writer Richard Curtis?

a) *Four Weddings and a Funeral*
b) *Bridget Jones' Diary*
c) *Notting Hill*
d) *Love Actually*

1. Elaine's

Her "little kicks" were eventually seen all over town after she recorded herself on a video that was copied and sold.

2. *The Larry Sanders Show*

The six-season show had 187 celebrity guests. Garry Shandling was offered deals for real talk shows but never accepted.

3. Chris Farley

His inept "motivational" speaker made the phrase "living in a van down by the river" iconic for a generation of viewers.

4. Ben Stein

Yale Law alumni, Stein's early profession was in politics, working as a speechwriter for Presidents Nixon and Ford.

5. *Bridget Jones' Diary*

When Grant finally heard the real Texas accent of his Bridget Jones' co-star Renee Zellweger he found it to be "very strange."

1. The premiere of which cop show drew public ire for showing a cast member's bare backside?

   a) *Law & Order*
   b) *Hill Street Blues*
   c) *NYPD Blue*
   d) *CSI*

2. Who walked away with an Oscar in 1997 for a film he wrote, directed and performed in?

   a) Cuba Gooding, Jr.
   b) Billy Bob Thornton
   c) Geoffrey Rush
   d) Anthony Minghella

3. What TV drama has been faulted for raising the expectations of real-life jurors and crime victims?

   a) *NCIS*
   b) *Law & Order*
   c) *NYPD Blue*
   d) *CSI*

4. On what kind of car was the *L.A. Law* license plate displayed at the start of each episode?

   a) Mercedes
   b) BMW
   c) Jaguar
   d) Porsche

5. Which British actor sparked a renewed interest in Shakespearean plays in film in the '80s and '90s?

   a) Anthony Hopkins
   b) Laurence Olivier
   c) Kenneth Branagh
   d) Leonardo DiCaprio

1. *NYPD Blue*

Profanity also contributed to the negative press. Over the years, the show was known for showing its actors semi-nude.

2. Billy Bob Thornton

He won the Oscar for adapting the screenplay for *Sling Blade*, for which he was also nominated for Best Actor.

3. *CSI*

Dramatic TV forensics cause some people to expect too much in actual court cases and crime solving – it's "the CSI effect."

4. Jaguar

Each episode began with a car trunk being shut, showing the plate. In the last seasons the Jag was upgraded to a Bentley.

5. Kenneth Branagh

Branagh played another well-known Shakespearean film actor, Laurence Olivier, in 2011's *My Week with Marilyn*.

1. Which documentary outgrossed all of the Best Picture nominees from the same year?

   a) *Earth*
   b) *Life*
   c) *March of the Penguins*
   d) *Born to Be Wild*

2. What candy did E.T. love?

   a) M&M's
   b) Skittles
   c) gumdrops
   d) Reese's Pieces

3. Who was Tim "The Tool Man" Taylor's arch nemesis on *Home Improvement*?

   a) Bob Vila
   b) his assistant Al
   c) his neighbor Wilson
   d) John the handyman

4. What character in Disney's *Winnie the Pooh* cartoons was not in A. A. Milne's books?

   a) Tigger
   b) Eeyore
   c) Gopher
   d) Piglet

5. Which Disney film had the most success come Oscar night?

   a) *Toy Story 3*
   b) *Up*
   c) *Beauty and the Beast*
   d) *Mary Poppins*

1. *March of the Penguins*

The French film stimulated heated debates in America on creationism and family values, but it was popular nonetheless.

2. Reese's Pieces

The candy's popularity skyrocketed after the film's release. Hershey's profits rose 65% in 1983.

3. Bob Vila

Electricity, fire, printed instructions and power tools were also enemies of his ambition for "more power."

4. Gopher

The first book had Pooh, Piglet, Owl, Rabbit, gloomy Eeyore, Kanga and little Roo. Tigger first appeared in the sequel.

5. *Mary Poppins*

Walt Disney holds the Academy record for most nominations (59) and wins (26). *Mary Poppins* alone won five of its 13 nods.

1. King Kong was scandalous because he peeled the clothes off what human subject-of-his-lust?

   a) Jean Harlow
   b) Fay Wray
   c) Mary Pickford
   d) Greta Garbo

2. *Cabin in the Woods* shared some of its monsters with which Joss Whedon cult TV series?

   a) *Firefly*
   b) *Buffy the Vampire Slayer*
   c) *Alias*
   d) *Dr. Horrible's Sing-Along Blog*

3. Which TV horror series was geared toward children?

   a) *Tales from the Crypt*
   b) *Are You Afraid of the Dark?*
   c) *Tales from the Darkside*
   d) *The Outer Limits*

4. Which daytime show featured supernatural characters before it became a norm for soap operas?

   a) *Guiding Light*
   b) *The Edge of Night*
   c) *Dark Shadows*
   d) *Kingdom Hospital*

5. *The Texas Chainsaw Massacre* was originally named after which villain?

   a) Mike Myers
   b) The Farmer
   c) Jigsaw
   d) Leatherface

1. **Fay Wray**

   Shot in 1933, the scene in which she visibly wore no undergarments and he peeled off her gown were not shown until 1971.

2. *Firefly*

   Whedon and Drew Goddard, who made *Buffy* and its spin-off *Angel*, wrote the *Cabin in the Woods* script together in just three days.

3. *Are You Afraid of the Dark?*

   Many episodes ended happily, to appease parents. R. L. Stine's popular *Goosebumps* kids' books were also adapted for TV.

4. *Dark Shadows*

   The 1960's soap featured vampire Barnabas Collins whom Johnny Depp adored as a kid. Depp plays him in a film remake.

5. *Leatherface*

   The human skeleton seen at the end was real – real skeletons from India were cheaper than prop skeletons in the U.S.

1. What program once boasted about its ratings on a billboard that read "#3 in Late Night"?

a) *The Tonight Show*
b) *The Late Show*
c) *Jimmy Kimmel Live!*
d) *The Colbert Report*

2. What trademark accessory was closely identified with CNN host Larry King?

a) bowtie
b) cufflinks
c) suspenders
d) pocketwatch

3. Which talk show host holds the record for the most Emmy nominations without a win?

a) Stephen Colbert
b) Bill Maher
c) David Letterman
d) Steve Allen

4. What late-night host made an appearance in *Forrest Gump* via a (partly) archived interview?

a) Johnny Carson
b) Jack Paar
c) Merv Griffin
d) Dick Cavett

5. Which host's autobiography is named after his most prominent physical feature?

a) Milton Berle
b) Jay Leno
c) Bob Hope
d) Dick Cavett

1. *The Late Show*

Dave always ran second to Leno's *Tonight Show*, but when his ratings fell behind *Nightline*'s, he decided to celebrate it.

2. suspenders

He'll forever be remembered bespectacled, behind a desk, sans jacket, sleeves rolled, with bright suspenders on display.

3. Bill Maher

He had 11 nods for *Politically Incorrect*, and nine for *Real Time*. Two of his HBO comedy specials earned nods, too.

4. Dick Cavett

Cavett wore a wig and makeup to look as he did in the mid-'70s; footage of John Lennon was added through archival film.

5. Jay Leno

The title, *Leading with My Chin*, is inspired by his prominent jaw – a result of the rare genetic disorder, mandibular prognathism.

1. What article of clothing did Ennis keep as a reminder of Jack in *Brokeback Mountain*?

a) shirt
b) hat
c) jeans
d) coat

2. Before *The Artist* won in 2012, how many silent films had been Oscar's Best Picture?

a) none
b) one film
c) two films
d) four films

3. Screenwriter Nora Ephron voiced one of the radio callers in which film?

a) *You've Got Mail*
b) *Julie & Julia*
c) *When Harry Met Sally...*
d) *Sleepless in Seattle*

4. One of AFI's top romantic comedies was the offbeat story of death-obsessed Harold and:

a) Harriet
b) Maude
c) the Undertaker
d) Laura

5. Kay Thompson's fashion editrix opened Funny Face by urging her staff to "Think" what?

a) "Spring"
b) "Paris"
c) "Pink"
d) "Chic"

1. shirt

The two shirts sold on eBay for $101,100 and were later loaned to a Los Angeles exhibition to represent the historical and fictional Western LGBT community.

2. one film

The first and only other silent film winner, *Wings*, won in the Oscar's inaugural year. *The Artist* was the first winner since '61 to be entirely black and white.

3. *Sleepless in Seattle*

The romance flick had a pre-*Seinfeld* "Soup Nazi" reference: "he's the meanest guy in the world but he makes the best soup you've ever eaten."

4. Maude

Bud Cort wanted Greta Garbo to play *Maude*, but Ruth Gordon was cast instead. She couldn't drive, so the hearse was towed during car scenes.

5. "Pink"

Astaire and Hepburn's roles were based on two fashion luminaries: photographer Richard Avedon and model Suzy Parker.

1. Who was injured in a 1977 car crash, causing concern about his sci-fi franchise's future?

a) William Shatner
b) Christopher Reeve
c) Mark Hamill
d) Lee Majors

2. BadAstronomy praised what film for being funny and having mostly accurate astronomy facts?

a) *Armageddon*
b) *Mission to Mars*
c) *Tomb Raider*
d) *Men in Black*

3. What was the name of the baseball player-turned-doctor in *Field of Dreams*?

a) Terrence Mann
b) Archibald Graham
c) Ray Kinsella
d) Joe Jackson

4. Stanley Kubrick bought what song after his star sang it unscripted in *A Clockwork Orange*?

a) "Over the Rainbow"
b) "As Time Goes By"
c) "White Christmas"
d) "Singin' in the Rain"

5. Whose strange kidnapping motivated *The X-Files'* Mulder to solve paranormal cases?

a) his sister
b) his brother
c) his mother
d) his wife

1. Mark Hamill

He endured severe facial trauma and a seven-hour surgery just one day before he was set to film a final *Star Wars* scene.

2. *Men in Black*

Its humor might have been very different had it been directed by the first guy to whom it was offered: Quentin Tarantino.

3. Archibald Graham

Prior to their professional acting careers, Ben Affleck and Matt Damon were among the extras in the film's Fenway Park scene.

4. "Singin' in the Rain"

Despite claims, the film was never banned in Britain; Kubrick pulled it himself after receiving numerous death threats.

5. his sister

Samantha Mulder was kidnapped while watching *The Magician*, the same show Patty Hearst was watching when she was abducted.

1. Which actor refused the Best Actor Oscar he was awarded for playing a famed WWII general?

a) George C. Scott
b) Marlon Brando
c) Gregory Peck
d) John Wayne

2. Which war movie was the first film about the Vietnam War directed by a Vietnam veteran?

a) *Platoon*
b) *Apocalypse Now*
c) *Full Metal Jacket*
d) *Good Morning, Vietnam*

3. Which automaker sponsored a commercial-free 1997 TV broadcast of *Schindler's List*?

a) Ford
b) Chevrolet
c) Mercedes-Benz
d) Volkswagen

4. Portions of *Spartacus* were filmed in the San Simeon estate of which tycoon?

a) William Randolph Hearst
b) Andrew Carnegie
c) John Rockefeller
d) Cornelius Vanderbilt

5. What *Mourning Becomes Electra* American playwright did Jack Nicholson play in *Reds*?

a) Eugene O'Neill
b) Arthur Miller
c) Edward Albee
d) Tennessee Williams

1. George C. Scott

He refused the nomination and later the award, stating the Oscars was a "meat parade." He bequeathed the award to the Patton Museum, but it was never delivered.

2. *Platoon*

Oliver Stone based the film around a screenplay he wrote in 1976 that recounted his personal experience in the war. It took him 10 years to get it approved by a studio.

3. Ford

Roman Polanski, whose mother died in Auschwitz, was offered the role of director but declined, stating he wasn't quite ready to tackle the Holocaust.

4. William Randolph Hearst

Scenes from *The Godfather* were also filmed at the estate. Hearst's life story was the inspiration for Orson Welles' 1941 drama, *Citizen Kane*.

5. Eugene O'Neill

Reds made Warren Beatty one of two men to get Oscar nods for writing, directing, acting and producing the same film.

1. Which two Brits have appeared in the *Harry Potter* and *James Bond* film franchises?

   a) Ralph Fiennes & Judi Dench
   b) John Cleese & Maggie Smith
   c) John Cleese & Ralph Fiennes
   d) Maggie Smith & Gary Oldman

2. Who ranked second among AFI's greatest heroes and *TIME*'s greatest fictional characters?

   a) Harry Potter
   b) James Bond
   c) Sherlock Holmes
   d) Indiana Jones

3. Who did **not** turn down the role of John McClane in *Die Hard* before Bruce Willis got it?

   a) Richard Gere
   b) Sylvester Stallone
   c) Mel Gibson
   d) Tom Selleck

4. Who robbed banks in *Bonnie & Clyde*, braved *The Poseidon Adventure* and played Lex Luthor?

   a) Warren Beatty
   b) Gene Hackman
   c) Roddy McDowall
   d) Marlon Brando

5. Roy Hobbs' baseball philosophy, cinematic swing and #9 uniform number were modeled on who?

   a) Joe DiMaggio
   b) Ted Williams
   c) Lou Gehrig
   d) Shoeless Joe Jackson

1. John Cleese & Ralph Fiennes

Cleese was Bond's Q and a Hogwarts ghost; Fiennes joined Bond in *Skyfall* and was, quite memorably, Harry's Voldemort.

2. Indiana Jones

He was bested by literary men on each list – Atticus Finch was AFI's greatest hero and Sherlock Holmes was *TIME*'s top character.

3. Tom Selleck

Most of the movie took place at night because Willis was busy filming his TV show, *Moonlighting*, during the day.

4. Gene Hackman

Voted "Least Likely to Succeed" by the Pasadena Playhouse, he has won 2 Oscars and 3 Golden Globes during his career.

5. Ted Williams

The beloved slugger said his goal was to make people say, "There goes Ted Williams, the greatest hitter who ever lived."

1. Which fast food chain did Morgan Spurlock visit every day for a month in *Super Size Me*?

a) Wendy's
b) McDonald's
c) Burger King
d) Big Boy

2. Marion Cotillard earned acclaim for her role in *La Vie en Rose*, a biopic about:

a) Coco Chanel
b) Édith Piaf
c) Maria Callas
d) Marie Antoinette

3. In what music mockumentary can a young Phil Collins and English model Pattie Boyd be spied?

a) *Zelig*
b) *This Is Spinal Tap*
c) *Help!*
d) *A Hard Day's Night*

4. Who delivered the introduction for each episode of HBO's *From the Earth to the Moon*?

a) Tom Hanks
b) Ron Howard
c) Neil Armstrong
d) Buzz Aldrin

5. Jennifer Lopez's *Selena* recreated the Tejano superstar's substantial concert in what city?

a) Santa Fe
b) Las Vegas
c) Houston
d) Phoenix

Biography

Answers

1. McDonald's

Six weeks after the film's release, McDonald's discontinued the supersize option but denied the movie as the cause.

2. Édith Piaf

She shaved back her hairline and shaved off her brows to in order to better resemble Piaf, who was just 4 ft. 9 in.

3. *A Hard Day's Night*

The kids chasing the band were real fans unleashed to shoot the scene; George's fall and near-trampling were also real.

4. Tom Hanks

The show featured many cast members of *Apollo 13*. Bryan Cranston (Buzz) was also Gus Grissom in Hanks' *That Thing You Do!*

5. Houston

Production filled the San Antonio Alamodome with over 64,000 extras to recreate the original concert.

1. What did *The Honeymooners'* Ralph Kramden do for a living?

   a) security guard
   b) mailman
   c) bus driver
   d) police officer

2. Which "Lost Generation" artist does Gil **not** carouse with in *Midnight in Paris*?

   a) Ernest Hemingway
   b) F. Scott Fitzgerald
   c) Pablo Picasso
   d) John Steinbeck

3. What TV chef did Melissa McCarthy say was the model for her *Bridesmaids* character Megan?

   a) Mario Batali
   b) Guy Fieri
   c) Paula Deen
   d) Rachael Ray

4. *O Brother, Where Art Thou?* gave a screenwriting credit to which classic author?

   a) Virgil
   b) Aeschylus
   c) Homer
   d) Plato

5. Bill Murray had to get rabies shots after being bitten by a large rodent on which film set?

   a) *Caddyshack*
   b) *Groundhog Day*
   c) *Rushmore*
   d) *Ghostbusters*

Comedy
Answers

1. bus driver

The Flintstones is based off the show. *The Honeymooners'* host nearly sued but didn't want to be "the guy who yanked Fred Flinstone" off TV.

2. John Steinbeck

In 1901 two women allegedly experienced a real time slip, where they suddenly stepped into pre-Revolution Versailles.

3. Guy Fieri

Co-star Jon Hamm was once a drama teacher in Missouri, where Ellie Kemper (naive bridesmaid Becca) was his student.

4. Homer

The Coens loosely based the plot on Homer's *The Odyssey*; Clooney's character was named Ulysses, after Homer's hero.

5. *Groundhog Day*

He faced a gopher in *Caddyshack*, but it was only a hand puppet. The rodent on the *Groundhog Day* set was very real (and a biter).

1) Tom Cruise's *Risky Business* led to a surge in sales of what?

a) white socks
b) pink button-down shirts
c) Wayfarer sunglasses
d) men's white briefs

2) Which TV Angel turned down the *Kramer vs. Kramer* role that won Meryl Streep an Oscar?

a) Farrah Fawcett
b) Kate Jackson
c) Jaclyn Smith
d) Cheryl Ladd

3) Ricky Gervais took credit for whose Golden Globe by noting he suggested Holocaust movies to her?

a) Vera Farmiga
b) Meryl Streep
c) Hilary Swank
d) Kate Winslet

4) Why was "mad as hell" newsman Howard Beale killed in *Network*?

a) his boss couldn't control him
b) he was crazy
c) a fan assassinated him
d) he had lousy ratings

5) Which caper won Best Picture just moments after a streaker ran behind David Niven at the 1974 Oscars?

a) *The Sting*
b) *Paper Moon*
c) *Chinatown*
d) *Murder on the Orient Express*

1. Wayfarer sunglasses

Risky Business made a star out of Cruise and sent the Wayfarer' sales from 18,000 units in 1982 to 360,000 in 1983.

2. Kate Jackson

Charlie's Angels producer Spelling couldn't shift the show's schedule to give her time off. It was Streep's first Oscar.

3. Kate Winslet

The quip was in reference to Winslet's appearance on Gervais' show *Extras* in 2005, on which she joked she planned on securing an Oscar with a Holocaust role.

4. he had lousy ratings

The daughter of newsman Walter Cronkite had a role in the award-winning film, playing kidnapped heiress Mary Ann Gifford.

5. *The Sting*

Evidence suggests that the stunt was planned. The streaker, photographer Robert Opel, was murdered 5 years later in San Francisco during an art gallery robbery.

1. What did Snape long to teach at Hogwarts, finally landing the position in *The Half-Blood Prince*?

a) Potions
b) Charms
c) Transfiguration
d) Defence Against the Dark Arts

2. Which children's show was originally banned in Mississippi when it began airing?

a) *Sesame Street*
b) *Flipper*
c) *The Electric Company*
d) *Fat Albert*

3. *Pee-Wee's Playhouse* has long been rumored to have been the creation of what comedian?

a) Steve Martin
b) David Letterman
c) Andy Kaufman
d) George Carlin

4. When the *Saved By the Bell* girls formed a pop group, what were they called?

a) The Tigeresses
b) Hot Sundae
c) The Excitations
d) Flaming Hearts

5. What was the name of the cat that belonged to Cinderella's stepmother?

a) Lucifer
b) Hades
c) Christopher
d) Dexter

1. Defence Against the Dark Arts

Alan Rickman (Snape) was privy to secrets of Snape's personal history that no one else knew until the final book was published.

2. *Sesame Street*

Even in 1969 the interracial cast was considered controversial in Mississippi and a state commission voted to ban it.

3. Andy Kaufman

Paul Reubens maintains his show was always separate from Kaufman's. Cyndi Lauper sang the Playhouse theme.

4. Hot Sundae

The burden of school and rehearsals drove Jessie to develop a horrifying addiction to over-the-counter caffeine pills.

5. Lucifer

June Foray, who voiced Lucifer, also gave voice to the Grinch's Cindy Lou Who and Rocky the Flying Squirrel.

1. Which Stephen King-inspired show contains many Stephen King references, such as his novel *Misery*?

   a) *Fringe*
   b) *Haven*
   c) *American Horror Story*
   d) *Millennium*

2. What was the first sign of impending trouble in *The Ring*?

   a) a videotape
   b) a phone call
   c) a letter
   d) a book

3. The miniseries *It*, based on Stephen King's novel of the same name, vilified what?

   a) a dentist
   b) a lizard
   c) a clown
   d) a snake

4. How does Claudia trick Lestat, leading to his supposed death in *Interview with a Vampire*?

   a) luring him into sunlight
   b) nailing him into a coffin
   c) giving him blood from corpses
   d) poisoning his wine

5. The first season of *American Horror Story* featured what bizarre figure?

   a) a headless male ghost
   b) a glowing male apparition
   c) a man comprised of water
   d) a rubber man

1. Haven

Set in the fictive Haven, Maine (itself a King creation), it also has a character who recently left Shawshank prison.

2. a videotape

The eerie *Ring* video was initially used as the trailer to promote the film and did not even mention the movie in its first broadcasts.

3. a clown

Coulrophobia, a fear of clowns, is medically recognized. *It* embodied this very real phobia with its sadistic clown "Pennywise."

4. giving him blood from corpses

She offers him the blood of twins she secretly poisoned with laudanum – blood from a dead body is fatal to a vampire.

5. a rubber man

The show has a novel approach: each season stands alone. The second season got an almost entirely new cast and plot.

1. Who was the celebrity guest on the only un-aired episode of *The Rosie O'Donnell Show*?

   a) Tom Selleck
   b) Christopher Walken
   c) O.J. Simpson
   d) Michael Jackson

2. Whose career was not launched by *The Daily Show*?

   a) Ed Helms
   b) Steve Carrell
   c) Amy Poehler
   d) Stephen Colbert

3. Whose *MTV Unplugged* album earned him six Grammys and over 10 million records sold?

   a) Tony Bennett
   b) Eric Clapton
   c) Paul McCartney
   d) Nirvana

4. What chatfest host said in 2011 she looked forward to playing her own sister in a sitcom?

   a) Chelsea Handler
   b) Rosie O'Donnell
   c) Sara Gilbert
   d) Ellen DeGeneres

5. Discovery Channel's week-long tribute to what animal greets an eager audience each year?

   a) lion
   b) dolphin
   c) elephant
   d) shark

1. Christopher Walken

Rosie refers to it as "The Scary Show." It was the only one out of her 1,193 episodes prohibited from broadcasting.

2. Amy Poehler

Colbert, who received an eponymous spin-off, has appeared on *The Daily Show* more than anyone, short of Jon Stewart.

3. Eric Clapton

He rearranged his music for the acoustic environment, giving many of his songs, like "Layla," a whole new identity.

4. Chelsea Handler

She noted that they couldn't use her sister's real name – "for legal reasons so that my own family can't sue me."

5. shark

Social media clamor each year as the awesome and gruesome marathon "Shark Week" nears, which has been airing since 1987.

1. *Love Story*'s Oliver Barrett was based on which pair of real-life Harvard roommates?

a) Dustin Hoffman & Gene Hackman
b) Robin Williams & Chris Reeve
c) Al Gore & Tommy Lee Jones
d) Robert Redford & Harrison Ford

2. *Gone with the Wind*'s Vivien Leigh hoped to star in which other romantic epic in 1939?

a) *Casablanca*
b) *Rebecca*
c) *Romeo & Juliet*
d) *Wuthering Heights*

3. Which Parisian painter took part in the tragic musical love affair, *Moulin Rouge*!?

a) Pablo Picasso
b) Claude Monet
c) Henri de Toulouse-Lautrec
d) Vincent Van Gogh

4. What did Clark Gable choose **not** to wear in *It Happened One Night*, causing the item's sales to plunge?

a) French-cuff shirts
b) neckties
c) razors
d) undershirts

5. *Ghost* put what ballad back on the charts 25 years after the song was first released?

a) "Unchained Melody"
b) "Stand By Me"
c) "Son of a Preacher Man"
d) "Can't Help Falling Love"

1. Al Gore & Tommy Lee Jones

In addition to having the lead character based on him, the film is also Jones' first. He graduated *cum laude* from Harvard in 1969 – *Love Story* was released in 1970.

2. *Wuthering Heights*

Leigh's real-life partner, Laurence Olivier, was already cast as Heathcliff. The studio execs opted to go with Merle Oberon for the role of Catherine instead of her.

3. Henri de Toulouse-Lautrec

Constant crouching to meet the artist's short stature put John Leguizamo in physical therapy for weeks after the film.

4. undershirts

He went without an undershirt because it interrupted the comedic delivery of his dialogue, unintentionally inspiring a trend.

5. "Unchained Melody"

The primary reason Demi Moore got the lead role was because she could cry out of each eye, independently, on cue.

1. To what city did *Angel* move after he left *Buffy* in Sunnydale?

a) New York
b) Los Angeles
c) Chicago
d) San Francisco

2. What western movie actor's name did Marty borrow in 1885 in *Back to the Future Part III*?

a) John Wayne
b) Gary Cooper
c) Clint Eastwood
d) Robert Redford

3. What sci-fi debacle won "worst drama" of the Razzie awards' first 25 years (1980-2004)?

a) *Star Wars: Episode II*
b) *Armageddon*
c) *Wild Wild West*
d) *Battlefield Earth*

4. Which star of *Planet of the Apes* was in both the 1968 original and 2001 reboot?

a) Roddy McDowall
b) Mark Wahlberg
c) Charlton Heston
d) Kris Kristofferson

5. Who campaigned for and won a recurring role as a *Star Trek: The Next Generation* bar-keep?

a) Ashley Judd
b) Whoopi Goldberg
c) Kirstie Alley
d) Jason Alexander

1. Los Angeles

When *Angel* was canceled despite high ratings, fans fittingly organized a blood drive to urge the WB to reconsider.

2. Clint Eastwood

During the hanging scene set in 1885, Michael J. Fox was accidentally hung and lost consciousness for several minutes.

3. *Battlefield Earth*

It's tied with *Showgirls* for third worst picture since 1980. Forest Whitaker expressed regret for even being part of it.

4. Charlton Heston

The original had the highest makeup budget in film history (adjusted for inflation); makeup was 17% of the total cost.

5. Whoopi Goldberg

A fan of the original series, she played Guinan from Seasons 2-6 of the second series and appeared in two *Star Trek* films.

1. Who wrote *How I Went to Africa with Bogart, Bacall and Huston and Almost Lost My Mind*?

   a) Ingrid Bergman
   b) Ava Gardner
   c) Joan Crawford
   d) Katharine Hepburn

2. In which country did Lt. Colonel Nicholson and Commander Shears build *The Bridge on the River Kwai*?

   a) Japan
   b) Thailand
   c) China
   d) Korea

3. Who or what was *The General*, the recipient of Buster Keaton's adoration?

   a) his general, Robert E. Lee
   b) President Abraham Lincoln
   c) his locomotive
   d) a giant clock

4. Jack Palance memorably did one-armed pushups while accepting an Oscar for which Western?

   a) *Shane*
   b) *The Desperados*
   c) *The Searchers*
   d) *City Slickers*

5. A Bonanza star's death became part of the show – a TV first – when what character died?

   a) Ben
   b) Little Joe
   c) Hoss
   d) Adam

1. Katharine Hepburn

The African Queen's cast faced dysentery, Black Mambas, herds of beasts and natives who thought the crew were cannibals.

2. Thailand

The fiction-based film used the real Burma Railway – the same place Japanese POWs in WWII were forced to build a bridge.

3. his locomotive

Initially panned, the silent film is now regarded as an all-time great. The Texas locomotive, which was crashed into the river for the movie, remained there until WWII.

4. *City Slickers*

Billy Crystal saw his first film at the age of seven when jazz icon Billie Holliday took him to *Shane*, also starring Palance.

5. Hoss

The West Wing, *NewsRadio*, *8 Simple Rules for Dating My Daughter*, *Mad Men* and even *Sesame Street* have integrated the deaths of castmates into storylines.

1. Which German film was the most expensive movie of the Silent Era?

a) *Svengali*
b) *Metropolis*
c) *Mata Hari*
d) *Nosferatu*

2. What surprise does Glenn Close leave on the stove for Michael Douglas in *Fatal Attraction*?

a) a human head
b) his daughter's pet rabbit
c) burned photos of his wife
d) his daughter's pet kitten

3. From which organism did *Jurassic Park* scientists extract dinosaur DNA?

a) lizards
b) snakes
c) chickens
d) mosquitos

4. What *Speed 2* actor was chided for lacking Keanu Reeves' "passion, fire and intellect"?

a) Sandra Bullock
b) Willem Dafoe
c) Jason Patric
d) Jeff Daniels

5. Which James Bond film marked the first franchise appearance of the Aston Martin?

a) *Dr. No*
b) *Goldfinger*
c) *From Russia with Love*
d) *Thunderball*

1. *Metropolis*

The five million mark film, which employed more than 37,000 extras, was reportedly one of Hitler's favorite movies.

2. his daughter's pet rabbit

In the original ending, Close kills herself with a knife that has Douglas' prints all over it, framing him for murder.

3. mosquitos

Tim Burton was considered to direct the movie until the film rights went to Steven Spielberg, who was writer Michael Crichton's first choice.

4. Jason Patric

Bullock called it "the biggest piece of crap ever made," but she did it to get funding for her film project *Hope Floats*.

5. *Goldfinger*

2012' *Skyfall* marked its ninth appearance. Aston Martin paid $70 million to be in *Die Another Day* a decade earlier.

1. What biographical drama had to re-shoot battles because some extras had sunglasses on?

   a) *Lincoln*
   b) *Lawrence of Arabia*
   c) *Bonnie & Clyde*
   d) *Braveheart*

2. What rock & roll biography was criticized for inaccuracies and inspired a rebuttal documentary?

   a) *Great Balls of Fire*
   b) *The Buddy Holly Story*
   c) *La Bamba*
   d) *Walk the Line*

3. What film faced controversy when people learned that the main character was a former Nazi?

   a) *A Beautiful Mind*
   b) *The Pianist*
   c) *Seven Years in Tibet*
   d) *Ed Wood*

4. *The Great White Hope* was based on the travails of which American boxer?

   a) Jack Johnson
   b) Jake LaMotta
   c) Sugar Ray Leonard
   d) Gene Tunney

5. Which celebrated Queen of England did Katharine Hepburn portray in *The Lion in Winter*?

   a) Elizabeth I
   b) Victoria
   c) "Bloody" Mary I
   d) Eleanor of Aquitaine

Biography
Answers

1. *Braveheart*

Descendants of William Wallace still residing in Scotland served as extras throughout the movie.

2. *The Buddy Holly Story*

Paul McCartney made *The Real Buddy Holly Story* 7 years later, which featured rock luminaries like Keith Richards.

3. *Seven Years in Tibet*

Brad Pitt's German accent in the film was ranked the third-worst movie accent ever by *Empire* magazine.

4. Jack Johnson

The original play won a Pulitzer. Johnson's friend Redd Foxx refused to take part because he felt it was inaccurate.

5. Eleanor of Aquitaine

Her portrayal tied her for Oscar's Best Actress with *Funny Girl*'s Barbra Streisand – 1 of only 2 ties in Oscar history.

1. *Clueless* featured two girls named after which 1970s divas who "now do infomercials"?

a) Carly Simon & Diana Ross
b) Cher & Donna Summer
c) Dionne Warwick & LaBelle
d) Cher & Dionne Warwick

2. What did Charlotte's first *Sex and the City* husband-to-be say when she suggested they wed?

a) "Okie-dokie."
b) "Alrighty."
c) "Yeah."
d) "Sure."

3. Cameron Crowe based *Almost Famous* and what other movie on his past *Rolling Stone* articles?

a) *Jerry Maguire*
b) *Say Anything...*
c) *Fast Times at Ridgemont High*
d) *Elizabethtown*

4. What was Clark hoping to buy with the bonus check that didn't come in *Christmas Vacation*?

a) new car
b) swimming pool
c) family vacation
d) his family's presents

5. Who attended a press screening for *The Devil Wears Prada* dressed in head-to-toe Prada?

a) Anna Wintour
b) Meryl Streep
c) Anne Hathaway
d) Miuccia Prada

1. Cher & Dionne Warwick

In the debate class scene, Silverstone genuinely mispronounced "Haitians"; the director wouldn't let the crew tell her.

2. "Alrighty."

Kim Cattrall declined the role of Samantha twice before finally accepting. She stayed on 'til the end, even despite her strained relationship with Sarah Jessica Parker.

3. *Fast Times at Ridgemont High*

While on the assignment that inspired *Fast Times*, he met a student, Geraldine Chapman, who partly inspired Penny Lane.

4. swimming pool

The movie's assistant director, Frank Capra III, was the namesake grandson of the director of *It's a Wonderful Life*.

5. Anna Wintour

The editrix reportedly threatened to ban designers from *Vogue* if they were in the film. Spokespeople later denied this claim.

1. Whose career was launched by portraying the teen trials and tribulations of Angela Chase?

   a) Winona Ryder
   b) Sarah Michelle Gellar
   c) Katie Holmes
   d) Claire Danes

2. Which 2008 film was shot in NY Catholic schools and received four Oscar nods for acting?

   a) *Revolutionary Road*
   b) *Doubt*
   c) *Changeling*
   d) *Milk*

3. What was the name of the amateur sleuth played by Angela Lansbury on *Murder She Wrote*?

   a) Katherine Beckett
   b) Jennifer Hart
   c) Jessica Fletcher
   d) Vanessa Potts

4. What did *Breaking Bad's* Walter White do professionally before he became a drug kingpin?

   a) chemistry teacher
   b) computer technician
   c) pharmacist
   d) doctor

5. *La Dolce Vita* is best-remembered for a scene shot in which iconic location?

   a) Trevi Fountain
   b) Colosseum
   c) Vatican
   d) Spanish Steps

Drama
Answers

1. Claire Danes

The teen anguish was not lost on adults – the show was listed among *TIME*'s 100 best TV shows.

2. *Doubt*

All of *Doubt*'s main actors received a nomination: Meryl Streep, Philip Seymour Hoffman, Amy Adams and Viola Davis. They share 25 total Oscar nods.

3. Jessica Fletcher

The mystery writer-turned-detective never drove – she always rode a bike, took a cab, or hitched a ride with someone.

4. chemistry teacher

Show creator, Vince Gilligan, stated that his overarching aim was to turn Walt's character from Mr. Chips into Scarface. He also defined "breaking bad" as "to raise hell."

5. Trevi Fountain

Mastroianni was so cold in the fountain that even a wetsuit under his clothes didn't help. He downed a whole bottle of vodka to warm up, and was drunk during the shoot.

1. *Reading Rainbow* was the only program to ever show bloopers from what other program?

    a) *Mister Rogers' Neighborhood*
    b) *Star Trek: The Next Generation*
    c) *Sesame Street*
    d) *The Cosby Show*

2. Which cartoon did *TIME* choose as the most significant fictional figure of the 20th century?

    a) Mickey Mouse
    b) all four South Park kids
    c) Bart Simpson
    d) Bugs Bunny

3. Which of the *Teletubbies* did evangelist Jerry Falwell say was a subversive gay role model?

    a) Po
    b) Tinky Winky
    c) Laa-Laa
    d) Dipsy

4. In what former Route 66 town did Lightning McQueen find a home with the other *Cars*?

    a) Radiator Springs
    b) Transmission Falls
    c) Piston Town
    d) Engine City

5. In what country did *The Sound of Music* take place?

    a) Switzerland
    b) Germany
    c) England
    d) Austria

1. *Star Trek: The Next Generation*

The bibliophilic show was hosted by LeVar Burton, who played Lt. Commander Geordi La Forge on the *Star Trek* sequel.

2. Bart Simpson

A "brat for the ages," he was the only animated person listed. His famous prank calls diminished over the years as writers struggled to concoct new & funny names.

3. Tinky Winky

The triangle antenna and purple hue initiated his theory. "Teletubby Land" was filmed in Stratford-Upon-Avon, the home of Shakespeare.

4. Radiator Springs

A white car with an Apple logo and #84 was a nod to Pixar's past-owner Steve Jobs and his iconic Mac, released in 1984.

5. Austria

The ending wasn't accurate – walking over the mountains would have taken the real von Trapps near Hitler's estate in Germany.

1. Which horror movie's villain was named after famous real-life killers?

  a) *Child's Play*
  b) *The Amityville Horror*
  c) *Saw*
  d) *Scream*

2. What horror plot came to William Alland during an Orson Welles' dinner party?

  a) *Jaws*
  b) *Leviathan*
  c) *Swamp Thing*
  d) *Creature from the Black Lagoon*

3. What did the Nevadans in *Tremors* name the giant worms that were shaking the ground?

  a) "Gopher Slugs"
  b) "Graboids"
  c) "Death Worms"
  d) "Groundlings"

4. Which short-lived cult TV series is identified with the line, "Someone's at the door."?

  a) *Twin Peaks*
  b) *Millennium*
  c) *Carnivàle*
  d) *American Gothic*

5. The evil supernatural denizens of what hotel terrorize Jack Nicholson in *The Shining*?

  a) Mountain Pass Hotel
  b) Overlook Hotel
  c) Hyperion Hotel
  d) Hotel Colorado

1. *Child's Play*

The full name of murderous doll "Chucky" was Charles Lee Ray, for Charles Manson, Lee Harvey Oswald and James Earl Ray.

2. *Creature from the Black Lagoon*

The Gill-man bodysuit overheated easily. To keep cool, Ben Chapman hung out in the studio's backlot lake, where the crew would occasionally hose him down.

3. "Graboids"

They were partly based on the Mongolian Death Worm, a cryptid intestine worm that spits acid and shoots electric discharges.

4. *American Gothic*

Teen heartthrob Shaun Cassidy created the show that *Entertainment Weekly* later ranked as one of the 17 creepiest TV shows of all time.

5. Overlook Hotel

Even after seeing Robert De Niro in *Taxi Driver*, Kubrick still didn't think he could play *The Shining*'s lead psychotic enough. Robin Williams was also considered for the role.

1. What show offers to appraise people's belongings, in hopes of finding unknown treasure?

   a) *Hidden Treasures*
   b) *Trash to Treasure*
   c) *Antiques Roadshow*
   d) *Attic Gold*

2. Mike Rowe, the host of Discovery's *Dirty Jobs*, is also a spokesman for which carmaker?

   a) Chevrolet
   b) GMC
   c) Ford
   d) Saturn

3. What show makes a point to say that all of the food eaten on the program is FDA approved?

   a) *Top Chef*
   b) *Hell's Kitchen*
   c) *The Dog Whisperer*
   d) *Fear Factor*

4. Which reality show documents what is generally considered the most dangerous profession?

   a) *Ice Road Truckers*
   b) *Deadliest Catch*
   c) *Dog the Bounty Hunter*
   d) *Ax Men*

5. Which late-night talk show is filmed in a studio nicknamed the "Eagle's Nest"?

   a) *The Colbert Report*
   b) *Conan*
   c) *Late Night*
   d) *The Late Late Show*

1. *Antiques Roadshow*

One of the show's biggest findings was a Seymour card table, procured at a garage sale for $25. It later sold at Sotheby's for $541,500.

2. Ford

He enjoys poking fun at the ad partnership on the show, like complimenting people on their Ford trucks.

3. *Fear Factor*

On the Fear Factor menu: cow bile, coagulated blood, rancid dairy, fish eyes, African cave spiders and leeches.

4. *Deadliest Catch*

Commercial fishing is, by itself, the most dangerous job, but the show's Alaska crab fishing is the worst of the worst.

5. *The Colbert Report*

Colbert's word "truthiness" entered Webster's Dictionary in 2006. In 2011-12, his Super PAC raised over $1 million.

1. What Africa-set film imported U.S. lions because filming native animals was banned?

a) *The African Queen*
b) *Morocco*
c) *Out of Africa*
d) *Casablanca*

2. What actress (who's no stranger to musicals) did Rex Harrison want in *My Fair Lady*?

a) Audrey Hepburn
b) Judy Garland
c) Julie Andrews
d) Barbra Streisand

3. What does George offer Mary as he walks her home from the dance in *It's a Wonderful Life*?

a) the moon
b) a house
c) a diamond ring
d) the stars

4. AFI's top-rated romantic comedy is *Charlie Chaplin's City Lights* where he plays:

a) a construction worker
b) a blind man
c) a king
d) a tramp

5. What did Audrey Hepburn' *Sabrina* study while she was in Paris?

a) culinary arts
b) fashion design
c) painting
d) photography

Romance
Answers

1. *Out of Africa*

The stars were extremely anxious to shoot the scene in which Denys washes Karen's hair, as there were some very territorial hippos nearby.

2. Julie Andrews

Had Audrey Hepburn declined, it would have been offered to Elizabeth Taylor, who wanted the role desperately.

3. the moon

Stewart was anxious about his first post-war, on-screen kiss. It ended up being so passionate it had to be edited for the censors.

4. a tramp

The scene where he buys the blind girls' flower required 342 takes. Filming was halted when Chaplin decided to make a short film with Winston Churchill.

5. culinary arts

The male leads hated each other. Bogart wanted his wife, Lauren Bacall, to star in it, while Holden and Hepburn had a love affair.

1. George Lucas based Han Solo on which legendary godfather of the cinema?

a) Alfred Hitchcock
b) Francis Ford Coppola
c) Frank Capra
d) Buster Keaton

2. On what ship did *Mystery Science Theater 3000*'s mad scientists trap Joel?

a) Satellite of Love
b) Cylon Raider
c) Shadow Battlecrab
d) Torchship

3. What 21st century fantasy film was directed by the great grandson of the original book's author?

a) *Star Trek*
b) *Cloud Atlas*
c) *Lord of the Rings*
d) *The Time Machine*

4. What animal plays a supporting role in *The Green Mile*?

a) dog
b) cat
c) bird
d) mouse

5. The "Trouble with Tribbles" on *Star Trek* is that they only eat and do what other thing?

a) shed
b) breed
c) grow in size
d) corrupt navigation

1. Francis Ford Coppola

Christopher Walken and Sylvester Stallone were among the actors considered for the role before Harrison Ford landed it.

2. Satellite of Love

The set for the ship and robots were built exclusively out of toys and kitchen items the producers got at Goodwill.

3. *The Time Machine*

This is the only non-animated film directed by Simon Wells. As a Dreamworks storyboard artist he's helped bring films like *Shrek* and *Kung Fu Panda* to life.

4. mouse

Mr. Jingles was resurrected by the gifted inmate. By the end of the film, the mouse was at least 64 years old.

5. breed

They can destroy planets due to their excessive population and appetites. Tribble props have sold for as much as $1,200.

1. Which TV western popularized the phrase "Get out of Dodge"?

a) *Gunsmoke*
b) *Rawhide*
c) *Bonanza*
d) *Maverick*

2. Which famous WWII setting was the backdrop for the star-studded film, *The Thin Red Line*?

a) Iwo Jima
b) Normandy
c) Guadalcanal
d) Stalingrad

3. In *The Good, the Bad and the Ugly*, which star played the bandit ("the Ugly") character?

a) Clint Eastwood
b) Eli Wallach
c) Lee Van Cleef
d) Charles Bronson

4. Which war movie was almost titled *Once Upon a Time in Nazi-Occupied France*?

a) *Saving Private Ryan*
b) *Casablanca*
c) *Inglourious Basterds*
d) *Patton*

5. What surprising and disastrous end befell Walnut Grove in *Little House on the Prairie*?

a) they deserted it
b) they flooded it
c) they burned it down
d) they blew it up

1. *Gunsmoke*

Over the course of the long-running show, many guest actors "died" on the show – Gary Busey played the last fatality.

2. Guadalcanal

Among the cast: Sean Penn, Jim Caviezel, Nick Nolte, Adrien Brody, John Cusack, Woody Harrelson and George Clooney.

3. Eli Wallach

Eastwood wore the same poncho in all three of the films in which he was the "Man with No Name" and never washed it.

4. *Inglourious Basterds*

The Oscar-winning role played to the hilt by Christoph Waltz was originally intended for Leonardo DiCaprio.

5. they blew it up

The sets were actually blown up for the farewell episode. Every building went down except for the Ingalls' home, which was destroyed 20 years later in a California fire.

1. Which Hitchcock blonde is Jimmy Stewart's former cop hired to tail in *Vertigo*?

a) Grace Kelly
b) Kim Novak
c) Tippi Hedren
d) Eva Marie Saint

2. The brainwashed assassin in *The Manchurian Candidate* (1962) was a veteran of what war?

a) World War II
b) Vietnam War
c) Korean War
d) World War I

3. What film did Brad Pitt plan to quit if its shock ending was cut like studio execs wanted?

a) *Mr. and Mrs. Smith*
b) *Twelve Monkeys*
c) *Sleepers*
d) *Se7en*

4. Which star of *The Bourne Identity* was only onscreen for three minutes?

a) Julia Stiles
b) Chris Cooper
c) Clive Owen
d) Joan Allen

5. Brad Pitt' star-making role in *Thelma & Louise* originally belonged to what actor?

a) William Baldwin
b) Tom Cruise
c) Johnny Depp
d) Sean Penn

1. Kim Novak

The American Film Institute ranked *Vertigo* as the greatest mystery of all time and the ninth best film overall.

2. Korean War

The senator's plane was owned by the film's star, Frank Sinatra, who broke a finger while filming a fight scene.

3. *Se7en*

R. Lee Ermey, who played the police captain (and *Full Metal Jacket's* drill sergeant), auditioned for the John Doe role.

4. Clive Owen

Unlike James Bond and many other cinematic agents, Bourne's gadgets are real and could be acquired by an ordinary person.

5. William Baldwin

Baldwin gave up the small part to take the lead role in *Backdraft*, which Pitt was coincidentally trying to win.

1. Which documentary series featuring noteworthy people uses the tagline: "Every life has a story"?

   a) *Behind the Music*
   b) *Biography*
   c) *True Hollywood Story*
   d) *History Channel Profiles*

2. Two of only three movies ever allowed to film on the Notre Dame campus were *Rudy* and:

   a) *Breaking Away*
   b) *We Are Marshall*
   c) *A Beautiful Mind*
   d) *Knute Rockne, All American*

3. What band inspired "Stillwater" in Cameron Crowe's semi-autobiographical *Almost Famous*?

   a) The Allman Brothers Band
   b) The Rolling Stones
   c) Aerosmith
   d) Led Zeppelin

4. A movie about which U.S. president was called *The Big Liar* in Hong Kong?

   a) John F. Kennedy
   b) Bill Clinton
   c) George W. Bush
   d) Richard Nixon

5. Which period biopic director was very formal on-set, addressing his lead as "Mr. President"?

   a) Oliver Stone
   b) Steven Spielberg
   c) Tom Hooper
   d) Martin Scorsese

1. *Biography*

The show was originally broadcast on CBS from 1961-64, and featured figures like Helen Keller. A&E revamped it in '87.

2. *Knute Rockne, All American*

Joe Montana, who was on the team with the real Rudy, confirmed that the jersey scene never actually happened.

3. The Allman Brothers Band

Brad Pitt initially took the role of guitarist Russell Hammond, but later dropped out, stating he didn't understand the character.

4. Richard Nixon

Nixon's family denounced the Disney-studio produced film. Walt Disney's widow, a Nixon family friend, publicly apologized to them.

5. Steven Spielberg

Highly detailed in his historical recreation, he even used a recording of Lincoln's original pocket watch in the film.

1. Alternate titles *Owl-Stretching Time, Sex & Violence,* and *It's...* were all considered for which comedy series?

a) *Monty Python's Flying Circus*
b) *Arrested Development*
c) *Community*
d) *Saturday Night Live*

2. Which pal do "the three best friends anyone could have" lose in *The Hangover*?

a) Alan
b) Stu
c) Phil
d) Doug

3. *The Office's* top paper salesman Dwight Schrute farms what vegetable with great pride?

a) potatoes
b) beets
c) rutabagas
d) turnips

4. Will Ferrell really had to eat Buddy the Elf's sugary meals, including what on every dish?

a) caramel
b) chocolate sauce
c) maple syrup
d) whipped cream

5. On which sitcom did Lisa Kudrow play a ditzy waitress before finding fame on *Friends*?

a) *Frasier*
b) *Mad About You*
c) *Cheers*
d) *Seinfeld*

1. *Monty Python's Flying Circus*

When the *Python* cast lost funding for *Life of Brian*, Beatles lead guitarist George Harrison stepped in and personally financed the movie.

2. Doug

The director tried to talk the cast into letting him use real tasers on them until the studio's lawyers got wind of it.

3. beets

Four cast members kept their real names for the show: Angela, Oscar, Creed and Phyllis. Actors who play Jim and Ryan graduated high school together in '97.

4. maple syrup

Eating so much sugar gave Ferrell headaches throughout filming. The cotton balls he ate were actually cotton candy.

5. *Mad About You*

Her absent-minded *Mad About You* waitress was later made the twin sister of her equally spacey *Friends* character, Phoebe.

1. In which movie was Jim Carrey's onscreen wife doing product pitches in their everyday life?

a) *I Love You Phillip Morris*
b) *The Majestic*
c) *The Truman Show*
d) *Man on the Moon*

2. When Matt Damon barks "How do you like them apples?" in *Good Will Hunting*, what is he showing off to his foe?

a) a girl's phone number
b) World Series tickets
c) a check
d) a solved math equation

3. On which film set did Daniel Day-Lewis concern the crew by sharpening knives during breaks?

a) *There Will Be Blood*
b) *Gangs of New York*
c) *Lincoln*
d) *The Last of the Mohicans*

4. Who did not play a doctor on *St. Elsewhere?*

a) Denzel Washington
b) Mark Harmon
c) Ed Begley, Jr.
d) Robert Downey, Jr.

5. TV comedienne Mary Tyler Moore took a dramatic turn in which 1980 Oscar-winning film?

a) *Coal Miner's Daughter*
b) *Tess*
c) *Ordinary People*
d) *Norma Rae*

1. *The Truman Show*

It was a 24-hour show, so they had to sneak ads into Truman's life – like her pitch for the coffee they had each morning.

2. **a girl's phone number**

The movie credits contain a dedication to the Beat writers Allen Ginsberg and William S. Burroughs, who both died in 1997.

3. *Gangs of New York*

The "Method" actor only wore a thin, period coat on-set and got sick – doctors had to force him to take antibiotics.

4. **Robert Downey, Jr.**

The film contains several nods to producer Bruce Paltrow's daughter: "Dr. Gwyneth Paltrow" is intermitently paged over the PA system.

5. *Ordinary People*

She lost the Oscar to 28-year-old Mary Steenburgen; all four winners for acting were under 40 – an Oscar first.

1. Which Disney villain was #13 on Forbes' 2005 "Fictional 15" list of wealthiest characters?

 a) Captain Hook
 b) Jafar
 c) Cruella de Vil
 d) Snow White's Evil Queen

2. As evidenced by his accent, from where does Bugs Bunny hail?

 a) Atlanta
 b) San Antonio
 c) Brooklyn
 d) Canada

3. Who sells Wile E. Coyote the products he uses in his attempts to catch the Roadrunner?

 a) AMCO
 b) ACME
 c) ACE
 d) ACHE

4. *Wall-E* enjoys listening to the soundtrack of which famed movie musical?

 a) *Hello, Dolly!*
 b) *Mary Poppins*
 c) *Sound of Music*
 d) *The Wizard of Oz*

5. In what earlier Pixar movie did an orange clownfish appear before *Finding Nemo* was released?

 a) *Toy Story*
 b) *A Bug's Life*
 c) *Cars*
 d) *Monsters, Inc.*

1. Cruella de Vil

Valued at $1 billion, she beat Gordon Gekko and ranked below Monty Burns, Lex Luthor, Willy Wonka and Scrooge McDuck.

2. Brooklyn

He was born in 1940 in a bunny burrow under the Dodgers' Ebbets Field. The original actor who voiced Bugs had a Flatbush accent.

3. ACME

"ACME" stands for: A Company Making Everything. A 2003 film revealed Wile works there (but probably not as a demonstrator).

4. *Hello, Dolly!*

Wall-E won the Academy Award for Best Animated Feature and tied *Beauty and the Beast* for most Oscar nominations for an animated film (six).

5. *Monsters, Inc.*

He was a plush toy on Boo's couch. Luigi from *Cars*, drives by the dentist's office in *Finding Nemo*, while a kid in the waiting room is reading *The Incredibles* comic book.

1. Why was Marion Crane on the run in
   Psycho, which ultimately took her to the
   Bates Motel?

   a) she witnessed a murder
   b) she was wanted for murder
   c) she stole $40,000
   d) she was having an affair

2. Which actor in 12 *Monkeys* says, at the
   end of a fight scene, "All I see are dead
   people."?

   a) Christopher Plummer
   b) Bruce Willis
   c) Brad Pitt
   d) Madeleine Stowe

3. Who liked blonde film victims because
   they were "virgin snow" showing "bloody
   footprints"?

   a) John Carpenter
   b) Wes Craven
   c) David Lynch
   d) Alfred Hitchcock

4. What screenwriter's varied dramas
   and horrors always have a central death
   theme?

   a) Ryan Murphy
   b) Stephen King
   c) Alan Ball
   d) Chris Carter

5. Which horror film was notable for killing its
   biggest star in the first 15 minutes?

   a) *The Exorcist*
   b) *Psycho*
   c) *Scream*
   d) *Interview with the Vampire*

1. she stole $40,000

The 1957 Ford Sedan that Marion drove for part of the film was the same car used in *Leave It to Beaver*.

2. Bruce Willis

Terry Gilliam directed Willis not to use mannerisms that he'd long-since named "Willis acting clichés," such as his steely-eyed stare.

3. Alfred Hitchcock

Among his "Hitchcock blondes": Grace Kelly, Janet Leigh, Tippi Hedren, Eva Marie Saint and Kim Novak.

4. Alan Ball

Before *American Beauty*, *Six Feet Under* and *True Blood*, he started out by scripting sitcoms *Grace Under Fire* and *Cybill*.

5. *Scream*

Drew Barrymore chose the small role over the lead role, insisting her early death would make audiences think anything could happen.

1. What *Survivor* season divided castaways into the Saboga, Chapera and Mogo Mogo tribes?

a) *Survivor: Fans vs. Favorites*
b) *Survivor: Heroes vs. Villains*
c) *Survivor: All-Stars*
d) *Survivor: Borneo*

2. Which talk show host was known for her trademark red-framed eyeglasses?

a) Sally Jessy Raphael
b) Ricki Lake
c) Katie Couric
d) Kathie Lee Gifford

3. Which deli, near the Ed Sullivan Theater, did David Letterman frequent for *Late Show* gags?

a) Carnegie Deli
b) Katz's Deli
c) Hello Deli
d) Studio Deli

4. MTV launched in 1981 with the introduction: "Ladies and gentlemen...":

a) "...music television."
b) "...rock and roll."
c) "...the Buggles."
d) "...here is your MTV."

5. Who hosted their talk show from a hospital bed while recovering from a torn back ligament?

a) David Letterman
b) Johnny Carson
c) Jack Paar
d) Ellen DeGeneres

1. *Survivor: All-Stars*

Two people quit, there was a tribe swap and a consolidation before power couple Rob and Amber took the top spots.

2. Sally Jessy Raphael

In 2010 Oprah reunited her '80s & '90s chat contemporaries, including Sally, Phil, Geraldo, Ricki and Montel.

3. Hello Deli

Hello Deli's Rupert Jee was one of many Letterman featured players, joining Biff, Alan Kalter and intern Stephanie.

4. "...rock and roll."

Its music video and chat show format has grown to include many reality shows, to the chagrin of its early audiences.

5. Ellen DeGeneres

Just so no one would feel out of place, she replaced the studio's chairs with hospital beds for the audience members.

1. When U.S. star Cyd Charisse left *An American in Paris*, what French actress replaced her?

a) Brigitte Bardot
b) Catherine Deneuve
c) Jeanne Moreau
d) Leslie Caron

2. Who or what was "Baby" in Katharine Hepburn and Cary Grant's *Bringing Up Baby*?

a) a dog
b) a leopard
c) an orphaned infant
d) the couple's baby

3. *The Unbearable Lightness of Being* was set during which European political uprising?

a) Velvet Revolution
b) October Riots
c) Prague Spring
d) January Events

4. Which rom-com saw a secretary usurp her boss' job and boyfriend while the boss was away?

a) *When Harry Met Sally...*
b) *Moonstruck*
c) *Roxanne*
d) *Working Girl*

5. What unlikely actor did Warner Bros. announce as *Casablanca*'s star before Bogart was hired?

a) Mickey Rooney
b) Ronald Reagan
c) Edward G. Robinson
d) Charlie Chaplin

1. Leslie Caron

Malnourished during WWII, she tired easily, which was handled by only filming her every other day.

2. a leopard

It was such a box office failure that Hepburn was labeled "box office poison." In 2007 AFI ranked it the 88th best film.

3. Prague Spring

The U.S.S.R. banned the film so its people couldn't see the Soviet invasion of Czechoslovakia from the Czech perspective.

4. *Working Girl*

After an actor left abruptly, Kevin Spacey joined the cast and filmed his role in the same day.

5. Ronald Reagan

At the time, Reagan was fresh off of *Knute Rockne, All American* and was a decade away from his masterwork: *Bedtime for Bonzo*.

1. A *Blade Runner*'s job was to retire human-like androids that were called what?

a) Recognizers
b) Replicants
c) Mandroids
d) Evolvers

2. *The Wizard of Oz's* Yellow Brick Road is coiled with a second road that's what color?

a) red
b) blue
c) purple
d) green

3. M.C. Escher's art inspired the special effects of which Christopher Nolan fantasy?

a) *Batman Begins*
b) *Memento*
c) *Inception*
d) *The Prestige*

4. In what language did Liv Tyler deliver most of her *Lord of the Rings* dialogue?

a) Maori
b) Elvish
c) Elvin
d) English

5. Sigourney Weaver nicknamed her *Alien* character Ripley after which male action hero?

a) *The Terminator*
b) *Mad Max*
c) *John McClane*
d) *Rambo*

1. **Replicants**

Director Ridley Scott's end title sequence included previously unseen footage from Stanley Kubrick's *The Shining*.

2. **red**

The Tin Man was recast after the aluminum makeup made Buddy Ebsen sick, but his vocal, not Jack Haley's, is still in the film.

3. *Inception*

He used Escher's images of never-ending staircases as the basic idea for the *Inception* world that folded over on itself.

4. **Elvish**

Tolkein devised two dialects of Elvish: Quenya, which is partly based on Finnish, and Sindarin, partly based on Welsh.

5. **Rambo**

Director Ridley Scott originally wanted *Alien* to end with the alien ripping off Ripley's head and assuming her identity.

1. Which iconic big screen cowboy first visited the Old West on the series *Rawhide*?

  a) John Wayne
  b) Gene Hackman
  c) James Garner
  d) Clint Eastwood

2. Kathryn Bigelow became the first woman to win Best Director, for directing what war movie?

  a) *The Reader*
  b) *Letters from Iwo Jima*
  c) *The Hurt Locker*
  d) *The Pianist*

3. Which early Hollywood western star was killed when his own suitcase hit him in the head?

  a) Gene Autry
  b) Tex Ritter
  c) Roy Rogers
  d) Tom Mix

4. Which war movie required 13,000 re-enactors to dramatize a single battle?

  a) *Saving Private Ryan*
  b) *Gettysburg*
  c) *Patton*
  d) *Glory*

5. What war movie starred actors also known as "Ferris Bueller," "Westley" and "Malcolm X"?

  a) *The Thin Red Line*
  b) *Gettysburg*
  c) *Apocalypse Now*
  d) *Glory*

1. Clint Eastwood

Many future TV stars were *Rawhide* guests, including future Enterprise shipmates Leonard Nimoy and DeForest Kelley.

2. *The Hurt Locker*

She was nominated against her ex-husband James Cameron (for *Avatar*), beating him for Best Director *and* Best Picture.

3. Tom Mix

While driving he swerved suddenly, causing his suitcase (full of money and jewels) to fall. It shattered his skull and broke his neck.

4. *Gettysburg*

Sam Elliot was so in character that a production member had to run ahead of him warning extras to interact with him as if he was really General John Buford.

5. *Glory*

Almost 20 years later, Matthew Broderick discovered he's the descendant of a Union soldier, just like his Glory character.

1. In what car did Steve McQueen rip through the streets of San Francisco in *Bullitt*?

  a) Dodge Charger
  b) Pontiac GTO
  c) Ford Mustang
  d) Chevrolet Camaro

2. Which Hitchcock thriller ends with a chase scene across Mount Rushmore?

  a) *Vertigo*
  b) *To Catch a Thief*
  c) *North by Northwest*
  d) *Dial M for Murder*

3. On which TV show was the murder of Laura Palmer investigated?

  a) *Lost*
  b) *The X-Files*
  c) *Desperate Housewives*
  d) *Twin Peaks*

4. To whom did Jack Nicholson shout, "You can't handle the truth!"?

  a) Demi Moore
  b) Kevin Bacon
  c) Tom Cruise
  d) Kiefer Sutherland

5. Alec Baldwin, Harrison Ford, Ben Affleck and Chris Pine have all played what character?

  a) Indiana Jones
  b) Jack Ryan
  c) Han Solo
  d) James Kirk

1. Ford Mustang

The chase took three weeks to shoot. The city denied them access to the Golden Gate Bridge, where they hoped to film.

2. *North by Northwest*

Hitchcock wanted to film in the U.N. but didn't have approval; he sent Cary Grant in and secretly filmed it from across the street.

3. *Twin Peaks*

The short-lived cult hit centered around a murdered homecoming queen, the townspeople, and possible supernatural forces.

4. Tom Cruise

A Few Good Men was an Oscar nominee, as was Nicholson – his line ranked among the AFI's 100 most memorable quotes.

5. Jack Ryan

They have all portrayed the CIA analyst in a big-screen adaptation of the Tom Clancy character; Ford did it twice.

1. Which psychiatric affliction plagued the subject of *A Beautiful Mind?*

 a) bipolar disorder
 b) Tourette syndrome
 c) schizophrenia
 d) obsessive-compulsive disorder

2. *Confessions of a Dangerous Mind* chronicled the dual-career of a CIA hitman and host of:

 a) *Password*
 b) *The $64,000 Pyramid*
 c) *I've Got a Secret*
 d) *The Dating Game*

3. What film's director was not on-hand to accept his Oscar because he's a fugitive?

 a) *The King's Speech*
 b) *A Beautiful Mind*
 c) *The Pianist*
 d) *The Last Emperor*

4. What '81 Best Actor & Actress Oscar winners were accompanied by the people they played?

 a) Ben Kingsley & Jane Fonda
 b) Robert De Niro & Sissy Spacek
 c) Henry Fonda & Meryl Streep
 d) Dustin Hoffman & Sally Field

5. Paul Giamatti only had two days off during a six-month shoot for this biography.

 a) *Too Big to Fail*
 b) *Cinderella Man*
 c) *Man on the Moon*
 d) *John Adams*

Biography

1. schizophrenia

John Nash was a Nobel Laureate in Economics. In the movie one of his sons plays an orderly who drags him down a hospital hall.

2. *The Dating Game*

Chuck Barris claimed he orchestrated the show's prize vacations to cover up his CIA hits.

3. *The Pianist*

Harrison Ford accepted the award on behalf of Roman Polanski, who fled the country in 1978.

4. Robert De Niro & Sissy Spacek

It was an unprecedented evening as both lead awards went to two actors who had their real-life "characters" present in the audience.

5. *John Adams*

To stay true to the period, all of the actors' teeth (even the extras') were painted dark to depict age-related decay.

1. John Cleese's *A Fish Called Wanda* character Archie Leach has which film icon's birth name?

   a) Orson Welles
   b) Cary Grant
   c) Charlie Chaplin
   d) Laurence Olivier

2. Which versatile actor played three characters in Stanley Kubrick's iconic *Dr. Strangelove*?

   a) George C. Scott
   b) Slim Pickens
   c) Orson Welles
   d) Peter Sellers

3. What satire featured Leslie Nielsen, Kareem Abdul-Jabbar, and *Leave It to Beaver*'s mom?

   a) *Naked Gun*
   b) *The Poseidon Adventure*
   c) *Airplane!*
   d) *Blazing Saddles*

4. Who played in the mockumentary band Spinal Tap and voiced characters on *The Simpsons*?

   a) Christopher Guest
   b) Harry Shearer
   c) Michael McKean
   d) Rob Reiner

5. Which cinematic college comedy popularized toga parties?

   a) *Animal House*
   b) *Old School*
   c) *Revenge of the Nerds*
   d) *Back to School*

1. Cary Grant

Cleese thought that naming his character "Archie Leach" was as close to being like his hero Grant as he'd ever get.

2. Peter Sellers

The conclusion was originally drafted to include a pie fight in the War Room following the round of nuclear detonations.

3. *Airplane!*

The cast also included Lloyd Bridges, Ethel Merman, and Robert Stack – the ominous-toned host of *Unsolved Mysteries*.

4. Harry Shearer

He was also a *Saturday Night Live* "player" and writer at two separate times. Guest joined him for his second run.

5. *Animal House*

It popularized the gross-out comedy film genre. It was also the film debut of Kevin Bacon and *Raiders of the Lost Ark's* Karen Allen.

1. In *On the Waterfront* Marlon Brando laments that he "coulda been a contender" instead of what?

   a) a schmuck
   b) a loser
   c) a bum
   d) a failure

2. Which legal thriller and 1957 Best Picture nominee was made for TV before it was a film?

   a) *Witness for the Prosecution*
   b) *12 Angry Men*
   c) *Friendly Persuasion*
   d) *Anatomy of a Murder*

3. In what city did *Forrest Gump* tell his life story while waiting for a bus?

   a) Savannah
   b) New Orleans
   c) Birmingham
   d) Memphis

4. Which of the lead actors in *Goodfellas* also narrated the film?

   a) Joe Pesci & Robert De Niro
   b) Ray Liotta & Joe Pesci
   c) Paul Sorvino & Lorraine Bracco
   d) Ray Liotta & Lorraine Bracco

5. Who directed the first *Columbo* episode in 1971, four years before his first blockbuster?

   a) Martin Scorsese
   b) George Lucas
   c) Steven Spielberg
   d) Francis Ford Coppola

1. a bum

He regrets a boxing match that he threw and knows he'll forever be a bum. It was the AFI's third most memorable quote.

2. *12 Angry Men*

It aired on CBS as a live teleplay in 1954. It was adapted for film in 1957; only two of the 12 original men performed in both.

3. Savannah

Thanks to CGI technology, iconic figures like John Lennon and John Kennedy were able to play a role in the film. The ping pong ball was also CGI animated.

4. Ray Liotta & Lorraine Bracco

All of the *Goodfellas* actors knew mob roles well: Bracco was later in *The Sopranos*; De Niro won an Oscar for *The Godfather Part II*.

5. Steven Spielberg

In 1974 he won Cannes' Best Screenplay prize for *Sugarland Express*. A year later he made his first blockbuster, *Jaws*.

1. *In Back to the Future*, what was the name of Doc Brown's dog, circa 1955?

a) Einstein
b) Newton
c) Verne
d) Copernicus

2. *Bewitched*'s Elizabeth Montgomery played both Samantha Stephens and Sam's cousin:

a) Seraphina
b) Sabrina
c) Selestina
d) Serena

3. Which force was one of the necessary components for summoning *Captain Planet*?

a) "Love"
b) "Faith"
c) "Heart"
d) "Hope"

4. Which Academy Award did Walt Disney receive for *Snow White*?

a) Best Animated Short
b) Best Picture
c) Honorary Award
d) he didn't receive anything

5. What did *The Lady and the Tramp* eat on their date?

a) spaghetti with meatballs
b) hot dogs
c) cake
d) pizza

1. Copernicus

The first time machine device was going to be a refrigerator. Spielberg abandoned this idea, afraid kids would start climbing into their refrigerators at home.

2. Serena

She was credited as "Pandora Sparks" and many fans never caught on, frequently sending her fan mail. Jodie Foster and Helen Hunt tried out for Tabitha.

3. "Heart"

The other Planeteers represented one of the four elements. Tom Cruise initially agreed to voice the role of Captain Planet but dropped out.

4. Honorary Award

There wasn't yet a category for animation; they gave him a full-size statue and seven miniature statuettes.

5. spaghetti with meatballs

Walt Disney originally did not want to include the scene and its accompanying song, "Bella Notte," in the movie.

1. How many camp counselors did Jason Voorhees kill in the first *Friday the 13th*?

  a) none
  b) five counselors
  c) eight counselors
  d) ten counselors

2. In what city did Brad Pitt tell Christian Slater his story in *Interview with a Vampire*?

  a) Paris
  b) New Orleans
  c) San Francisco
  d) New York

3. *Halloween* star Jamie Lee Curtis acted in which other John Carpenter horror film?

  a) *Someone's Watching Me!*
  b) *The Fog*
  c) *The Thing*
  d) *Village of the Damned*

4. Which TV horror program is based on a comic book series?

  a) *True Blood*
  b) *Haven*
  c) *The Walking Dead*
  d) *American Horror Story*

5. *Snow White* and what early horror film were reportedly Hitler's favorite movies?

  a) *Dracula*
  b) *The War of the Worlds*
  c) *King Kong*
  d) *Frankenstein*

1. **none**

His mother killed eight counselors to avenge his supposed death at camp; he returned in sequels to avenge her death.

2. **San Francisco**

Christian Slater replaced River Phoenix in the reporter role after Phoenix died suddenly, just two weeks before filming began.

3. *The Fog*

The Fog shared a setting with *The Birds*: Bodega Bay. Curtis' arrival mirrors Tippi Hedren's in the Hitchcock classic.

4. *The Walking Dead*

It's the only zombie show to ever achieve mainstream success, with several Emmy nods and glowing reviews from AFI and *Newsweek*.

5. *King Kong*

Initially hoping to be an artist, Hitler failed the art academy's entrance exam twice. His early works include postcard views of Vienna and Disney watercolor paintings.

1. Who usually "Slow Jams the News" with Jimmy Fallon on *Late Night*?

   a) Tom Brokaw
   b) Seth Meyers
   c) Tina Fey
   d) Brian Williams

2. U.S. Congressman Sean Duffy was on the sixth season of *The Real World*, set in which city?

   a) Boston
   b) Miami
   c) San Francisco
   d) London

3. What nonfiction show dramatically chronicles only music luminaries?

   a) *Biography: Music*
   b) *The MTV Vault*
   c) *Behind the Music*
   d) *Billboard Profiles*

4. Despite the title, several stars of *Keeping Up with the Kardashians* have what surname?

   a) Lohan
   b) Jackson
   c) Jenner
   d) Hilton

5. Of the five *The View* co-hosts who have left the show, how many left on good terms?

   a) none of them
   b) one co-hosts
   c) two co-host
   d) three co-hosts

1. Brian Williams

President Obama filled in for him on one occasion, slow jamming about blocking Stafford Loan interest rate hikes.

2. Boston

He wed *Real World: San Francisco* castmate, Rachel Campos. They settled in Wisconsin where he was elected to Congress in 2010.

3. *Behind the Music*

The show's dramatic tone is a popular source of parody, inspiring spoofs like *SNL*'s legendary "More Cowbell" skit.

4. Jenner

Kim Kardashian ranked third in a *Playboy* poll on the most popular centerfolds, behind Marilyn Monroe and Pam Anderson.

5. two co-hosts

Debbie Matenopoulos was let go due to bad press; Star Jones announced her departure on-air; Rosie O'Donnell left amid conflict with producers.

1. Hilarity ensued when Alvy tried to handle what food in *Annie Hall*?

a) chicken
b) snails
c) onions
d) lobsters

2. What film star was shown on a website for Lacuna, a fictive company that erases memories?

a) Jude Law
b) Jim Carrey
c) Adam Sandler
d) Philip Seymour Hoffman

3. In *The Notebook* Allie emphatically urges Noah to declare that he, too, is what?

a) sorry
b) in love
c) a fish
d) a bird

4. What writer, experienced at adapting Jane Austen, edited the script for *Pride & Prejudice*?

a) Andrew Davies
b) Emma Thompson
c) Julian Fellowes
d) Tom Stoppard

5. Which *Sense and Sensibility* actor did the Jane Austen Society complain was too attractive?

a) Emma Thompson
b) Kate Winslet
c) Hugh Grant
d) Alan Rickman

1. lobsters

Boiling live lobsters is an inherently comical onscreen act. Amy Adams scored laughs in Julie & Julia while attempting the same dish.

2. Jim Carrey

To promote *Eternal Sunshine of the Spotless Mind*, a company site was created, showing his character's memory erasure.

3. a bird

Rachel McAdams auditioned for the role of Allie after receiving the script just a day before. Both her and Ryan Gosling were born in London, Ontario Canada.

4. Emma Thompson

The director had to wave a red flag so Matthew McFayden, who had poor vision, could find Keira Knightley in the mist.

5. Hugh Grant

Grant, an Oxford grad in English, thought Emma Thompson' screenplay was better than the original Jane Austen book.

1. What does Neo do that makes him such an attractive recruit for Morpheus in *The Matrix*?

   a) he's a hacker
   b) he's a police officer
   c) he's a skilled martial artist
   d) he lives "off the grid"

2. Before they made TV's *Twin Peaks* together, Kyle MacLachlan made *Dune* with which director?

   a) Ridley Scott
   b) David Lynch
   c) James Cameron
   d) John Waters

3. The *Fringe* Division is a branch of which U.S. government agency?

   a) NASA
   b) Secret Service
   c) CIA
   d) FBI

4. Spencer Tracy was the first choice to play the alien visitor in what iconic '50s sci-fi film?

   a) *The Day the Earth Stood Still*
   b) *Invasion of the Body Snatchers*
   c) *The Thing from Another World*
   d) *Forbidden Planet*

5. How did the aliens in *The Body Snatchers* (1956) come to Earth?

   a) bubbles
   b) flying saucers
   c) meteorites
   d) seed pods

1. he's a hacker

Will Smith, Tom Cruise and Nicolas Cage were originally offered the role of Neo, while Gary Oldman was considered for Morpheus.

2. David Lynch

Lynch turned down directing *Return of the Jedi* to make *Dune*, which Jack Nicholson was reportedly also interested in helming.

3. FBI

In the *Fringe* world's parallel universe, Humphrey Bogart did not star in *Casablanca* or *The Maltese Falcon*.

4. *The Day the Earth Stood Still*

Before the role went to Michael Rennie, it was offered to Claude Rains of *Casablanca*, *Lawrence of Arabia* and Hitchcock's *Notorious*.

5. seed pods

Jack Finney's original book has been adapted for film four times – 1956 was the first, followed by 1978, 1993 and 2007.

1. Which miniseries about a war took longer to make than the war itself lasted?

   a) *Band of Brothers*
   b) *The Civil War*
   c) *North and South*
   d) *The Winds of War*

2. *China Beach* opened to the strains of what Motown classic by The Supremes?

   a) "Someday We'll Be Together"
   b) "You Keep Me Hanging On"
   c) "Stop! In the Name of Love"
   d) "Reflections"

3. Re-runs of what sitcom, set during a war, were aired in Germany in place of *Seinfeld*?

   a) *F Troop*
   b) *M*A*S*H*
   c) *Hogan's Heroes*
   d) *McHale's Navy*

4. Which *M*A*S*H* character spent numerous seasons trying to "earn" a Section 8 designation?

   a) Maxwell Klinger
   b) Hot Lips Houlihan
   c) Radar O'Reilly
   d) Trapper John McIntyre

5. In *Homeland* Claire Danes portrays a counterterrorism agent afflicted with what disorder?

   a) post-traumatic stress disorder
   b) obsessive-compulsive disorder
   c) bipolar disorder
   d) schizophrenia

1. *The Civil War*

The Ken Burns documentary miniseries was the highest rated program in PBS history and won more than 40 major awards.

2. "Reflections"

Great reviews but low ratings led to cancellation. Dana Delaney won an Emmy for the show over a year after it ended.

3. *Hogan's Heroes*

German viewers simply didn't understand *Seinfeld*'s humor, but the campy WWII-set sitcom was unceasingly popular.

4. Maxwell Klinger

Known for donning women's dresses, he was initially written as a gay character. Writers later decided to make him a heterosexual who would do anything to leave.

5. bipolar disorder

Its debut season swept the Emmys, winning top drama, best actor and actress. President Obama cited it as his favorite show.

1. The title of *The Usual Suspects* was inspired by which classic film?

a) *The Godfather*
b) *Citizen Kane*
c) *Casablanca*
d) *Rear Window*

2. Before *The Hunger Games* what was the top-grossing action film with a woman as lead hero?

a) *Kill Bill Vol. 1*
b) *Alien*
c) *Salt*
d) *Lara Croft: Tomb Raider*

3. What did *Fight Club's* Tyler Durden make and sell?

a) soap
b) short films
c) explosives
d) artwork

4. Which James Bond film was scripted by children's author Roald Dahl?

a) *The Spy Who Loved Me*
b) *You Only Live Twice*
c) *Goldfinger*
d) *Dr. No*

5. Which film favorite produced the memorable lesson, "There's no crying in baseball!"?

a) *A League of Their Own*
b) *Bull Durham*
c) *Field of Dreams*
d) *Pride of the Yankees*

1. *Casablanca*

Claude Rains says, "Round up the usual suspects!" AFI listed it as one of the most memorable film quotes of all time.

2. *Lara Croft: Tomb Raider*

Angelina Jolie is the most successful female action star for her roles in *Lara Croft* and *Mr. & Mrs. Smith*, among others.

3. soap

The tagline was "Mischief. Mayhem. Soap." To prepare, the actors took lessons in boxing, Taekwondo and soapmaking.

4. *You Only Live Twice*

Many of Dahl's beloved books have hit the big screen, too: *Charlie and the Chocolate Factory*, *Fantastic Mr. Fox*, and *Matilda*.

5. *A League of Their Own*

Hanks berated a Peach with such ferocity for crying when it's "not allowed," that the umpire ejected him.

1. In which movie was Leonardo DiCaprio "arrested" by the man he was portraying?

a) *Titanic*
b) *The Aviator*
c) *Catch Me If You Can*
d) *The Basketball Diaries*

2. Which *J. Edgar* star said he took the role to avenge Hoover's real scrutiny of his family?

a) Leonardo DiCaprio
b) Armie Hammer
c) Ken Howard
d) Josh Lucas

3. Which role in *Chaplin* was played by a member of Charlie Chaplin's family?

a) Chaplin's last wife
b) Chaplin's mother
c) Chaplin's editor
d) Douglas Fairbanks

4. Julia Roberts had her first $20 million payday – a first for any actress – for what biopic?

a) *Michael Collins*
b) *Mona Lisa Smile*
c) *Eat Pray Love*
d) *Erin Brockovich*

5. What film-shoot kept Queen Elizabeth II from visiting the Forbidden City?

a) *The Last Emperor*
b) *Gandhi*
c) *Seven Years in Tibet*
d) *Out of Africa*

Biography
Answers

1. *Catch Me If You Can*

Real-life Frank Abergnale, Jr. had the pleasure of arresting his silver-screen self. He also reviewed the film to ensure authenticity.

2. Armie Hammer

His great-grandfather, Armand Hammer, was the head of Occidental Petroleum and had Soviet ties that drew Hoover's attention.

3. Chaplin's mother

Geraldine Chaplin, his oldest child with his last wife, Oona O'Neill, played her paternal grandmother, Hannah.

4. *Erin Brockovich*

The real Brockovich made a cameo in a restaurant scene, playing a waitress fittingly named, "Julia."

5. *The Last Emperor*

It's one of only three films to get more than five Oscar nods (nine) and win each category in which it was nominated.

1. Despite the title, where does much of the story in *Fargo* actually take place?

  a) Brainerd, MN
  b) Bismarck, ND
  c) St. Paul, MN
  d) Sioux Falls, SD

2. What aspect of *I Love Lucy* was considered controversial when it aired? .

  a) "Vitameatavegamin" drunkenness
  b) the interracial marriage
  c) Lucy's pregnancy
  d) Lucy working outside the home

3. What did *Juno* pack Paulie's mailbox with in an attempt to show her affection?

  a) orange chewing gum
  b) orange Tic Tacs
  c) Sunny D
  d) orange guitar picks

4. Which of Mike Myers' classic characters did not appear in recurring sketches for *SNL*?

  a) Wayne Campbell
  b) Dieter, of Sprockets
  c) Linda Richman
  d) Austin Powers

5. Which '80s movie featured "a brain, an athlete, a basket case, a princess and a criminal"?

  a) *Sixteen Candles*
  b) *The Breakfast Club*
  c) *St. Elmo's Fire*
  d) *Ferris Bueller's Day Off*

1. Brainerd, MN

Despite its disclaimer, the movie is not actually based on a true story. The Coen brothers added it so viewers would take the film seriously.

2. Lucy's pregnancy

In 1952 censors refused to let the actors utter the word "pregnant" onscreen, even though Lucy and Ricky were married.

3. Orange Tic Tacs

The film' screenwriter, Diablo Cody, a former stripper, won an Oscar for the screenplay – her first-ever script.

4. *Austin Powers*

One of his first acting jobs – at age 10 – was a commercial with *SNL* founding cast member Gilda Radner.

5. *The Breakfast Club*

John Hughes nearly fired Judd Nelson during filming. His refusal to work with the actor ruined the possibility for sequels.

1. *When Mr. Smith Goes to Washington*, he leads a 23-hour filibuster in court to prove he didn't want to build:

   a) an oilfield
   b) a coal mine
   c) a dam
   d) a factory

2. In which film did Keira Knightley wear a now-iconic green dress?

   a) *Pride and Prejudice*
   b) *Atonement*
   c) *Silk*
   d) *The Duchess*

3. Who played Betsy, the object of Travis Bickle's deranged fixation, in *Taxi Driver*?

   a) Jodie Foster
   b) Meryl Streep
   c) Tatum O'Neal
   d) Cybill Shepherd

4. Who was Don Draper before he borrowed the name of a fallen army buddy on *Mad Men*?

   a) Dan Jones
   b) Tom Morgan
   c) Dick Whitman
   d) Harry Williams

5. Where were the *Fried Green Tomatoes* served?

   a) Truvy's
   b) Sugar Baker's
   c) the Whistle Stop Cafe
   d) Piggly Wiggly

1. **a dam**

Jimmy Stewart and director Frank Capra re-teamed seven years later to make the equally beloved *It's a Wonderful Life*.

2. *Atonement*

InStyle named Keira's dress the best silver-screen gown of all time, beating out dresses that bedecked Audrey Hepburn and Marilyn Monroe.

3. **Cybill Shepherd**

The movie "inspired" John Hinckley, Jr. to attempt assassination on Ronald Reagan in the hope it would impress its teen star, Jodie Foster, with whom he was obsessed.

4. **Dick Whitman**

His secret history was spoofed on *30 Rock* – Kenneth admitted during a medical crisis that *his* real name was Dick Whitman.

5. **The Whistle Stop Cafe**

Comedienne Fannie Flagg wrote the original novel, which told the stories of female friends and, later, a murder mystery.

1. Inspired by a popular mid-century singer and actress, what is Miss Piggy's last name?

a) Reynolds
b) Holiday
c) Lee
d) Garland

2. Mickey Mouse was first introduced to audiences in a 1928 cartoon short entitled what?

a) *Whistle While You Work*
b) *A Mouse*
c) *Steamboat Willie*
d) *A Whistle and a Tail*

3. What kind of BB gun was Ralphie desperate to find under the tree in *A Christmas Story*?

a) Daisy
b) Winchester
c) Colt
d) Red Ryder

4. Harry Potter's ability to speak to snakes makes him fluent in what language?

a) Hissilitch
b) Parseltongue
c) Basilisk
d) Slytherinch

5. How many fingers did *Pinocchio* gain on each hand when he became a real boy?

a) one
b) two
c) none
d) he lost one

1. Lee

Director Frank Oz played Miss Piggy from 1976-'01. He has also given voice to Cookie Monster, Yoda, and Jeff Fungus in *Monsters, Inc.*

2. *Steamboat Willie*

After building an empire Walt Disney once said, "I hope we'll never lose sight of one thing – that it was all started by a mouse."

3. Red Ryder

He asked for the gun, by name, 28 times in the movie. The film inspired *The Wonder Years* and a rabid legion of fans.

4. Parseltongue

Voldemort was a Parselmouth; the piece of him in Harry gave him the ability. When Voldemort died so did Harry's ability.

5. one

He had three wooden fingers (and thumb) on each white-gloved hand, but magically lost the gloves and gained two fingers.

1. Where did the killer spiders in
   Arachnophobia originate?

   a) Congo
   b) Thailand
   c) Venezuela
   d) New Zealand

2. Where can the legendary horror film
   address 112 Ocean Avenue be found?

   a) Georgetown, Washington, D.C.
   b) Amityville, New York
   c) Mount Hood, Oregon
   d) Universal Studios, Los Angeles

3. Alfred Hitchcock suffered from ovophobia,
   which is a fear of what?

   a) things over his head
   b) flying
   c) eggs
   d) birds

4. What HBO series featured stand-alone
   episodes, allowing A-list stars and directors
   to do one-offs?

   a) *The Outer Limits*
   b) *Tales from the Crypt*
   c) *The Twilight Zone*
   d) *Perversions of Science*

5. What actor and future macabre film star
   made his screen debut in *Nightmare on
   Elm Street*?

   a) Brad Pitt
   b) Michael Keaton
   c) Skeet Ulrich
   d) Johnny Depp

1. Venezuela

Harmless Avondale spiders were used, as was a bird-eating tarantula that had to be handled by an expert to avoid bites.

2. Amityville, New York

Both *Amityville Horror* stars, James Brolin and Margot Kidder, did not believe the supposedly true story.

3. eggs

The maestro of suspense gave voice to a more common fear: sharks. He narrated the "Jaws" theme park ride.

4. *Tales from the Crypt*

Michael J. Fox, Tom Hanks, Brad Pitt, Daniel Craig, Kirk Douglas and Whoopi Goldberg were just some of the many contributors.

5. Johnny Depp

Depp tends to gravitate toward darker roles: *Edward Scissorhands*, *Sweeney Todd* and *Ichabod Crane* among them.

1. Who was ridiculed for asking Katharine Hepburn what kind of tree she'd like to be?

a) Katie Couric
b) Diane Sawyer
c) Barbara Walters
d) Meredith Viera

2. What talk show was awarded the dubious distinction of being *TV Guide*'s worst show ever?

a) *The Tom Green Show*
b) *The Chevy Chase Show*
c) *The Jerry Springer Show*
d) *The Howard Stern Show*

3. Which talk show host was, for four years, the son-in-law of author Kurt Vonnegut?

a) Phil Donahue
b) Maury Povich
c) Jerry Springer
d) Geraldo Rivera

4. Amid the 2010 *Tonight Show* debacle, ousted host Conan O'Brien's fans rallied, saying:

a) "I'm with Coco"
b) "Team Ginja Ninja"
c) "Ginger Power"
d) "It's Only Tonight with Conan"

5. Whose late-night show did Bill Clinton visit to play the saxophone in 1992?

a) David Letterman
b) Jay Leno
c) Arsenio Hall
d) Magic Johnson

1. Barbara Walters

Her accent and softball questions inspired a "Baba Wawa" impersonation by *SNL*'s Gilda Radner.

2. *The Jerry Springer Show*

Springer did not aim to be a smut peddler – the popular former mayor of Cincinnati was also a campaign aide to Robert Kennedy.

3. Geraldo Rivera

After Geraldo released his autobiography, Vonnegut stated he thought his former son-in-law had a few "screws loose."

4. "I'm with Coco"

Tom Hanks popularized the name during the second episode of *The Tonight Show*; Conan jokingly threatened to sue Hanks if it caught on.

5. Arsenio Hall

Clinton donned shades to play Elvis' "Heartbreak Hotel." The show was credited with boosting his status with young voters.

1. Where were Sam and Ted "The Geek" when she gave him her panties in *Sixteen Candles*?

   a) a party at Jake's house
   b) the school bus
   c) a school dance
   d) her house

2. What song did Lloyd Dobler play Diane when he held up the stereo outside her window in *Say Anything*?

   a) "In Your Eyes"
   b) "All for Love"
   c) "Solsbury Hill"
   d) "Every Breath You Take"

3. The two most Oscar-awarded films of the 1990s were *Titanic* and what other romantic drama?

   a) *Out of Africa*
   b) *The English Patient*
   c) *Shakespeare in Love*
   d) *Ghost*

4. What does *Edward Scissorhands* fittingly make for Winona Ryder to declare his affection?

   a) chains of paper hearts
   b) sculpted topiaries
   c) collages
   d) ice sculpture

5. Where does Richard Gere take Julia Roberts, bedecked in red, on a date in *Pretty Woman*?

   a) to a play
   b) to the opera
   c) to the symphony
   d) to a ball

1. **a school dance**

The guest that Sam's sister Ginny tried to sit down with during her wedding was played by John and Jim Belushi's mother.

2. **"In Your Eyes"**

When they filmed the scene, a Fishbone song was actually playing. "In Your Eyes" was added in post-production.

3. *The English Patient*

It won nine total awards in 1997, prompting Best Song winner Andrew Lloyd Webber (*Evita*) to thank *The English Patient* for being song-less.

4. **ice sculpture**

Ryder and Depp were engaged in real life, inspiring a "Winona Forever" tattoo that he changed to "Wino Forever" after they split.

5. **to the opera**

The opera was *La Traviata*, about a prostitute who's in love with a rich man. Roberts won the role after Brooke Shields was fired.

1. Which incarnation of *Doctor Who* often exclaimed "Allons-y!"?

a) the Eighth Doctor
b) the Ninth Doctor
c) the Tenth Doctor
d) the Eleventh Doctor

2. What show inspired a loyal following of "Browncoats" despite only running for 14 episodes?

a) *Pushing Daisies*
b) *Firefly*
c) *Veronica Mars*
d) *Farscape*

3. *Battlestar Galactica* is the fictional world to which this manufactured race belongs:

a) Sentinels
b) Cylons
c) Decepticons
d) Daleks

4. What was the profession of the man with the magic touch on *Pushing Daisies*?

a) baker
b) mortician
c) gardener
d) author

5. In *Alien*, the creature laid eggs in a victim's chest – a detail inspired by what insect?

a) spider
b) praying mantis
c) horsefly
d) wasp

1. the Tenth Doctor

The show, which defies TV logic by repeatedly recasting the leads, was ranked as one of *Entertainment Weekly*'s top cult show.

2. *Firefly*

A sci-fi/Western set in a time dominated by a U.S./China alliance, it was a short-lived triumph of unlikely pairings.

3. Cylons

The series started in the '70s and was reborn in 2004. The reboot introduced the pseudo-expletive "Frak!" into the lexicon.

4. baker

The show's cult following was crushed when the show was canceled with three episodes remaining in the second season.

5. wasp

Screenwriter Dan O'Bannon was inspired by personal nightmares of egg-laying spider wasps and wasp maggots eating their prey from the inside out.

1. In *Tropic Thunder* who stated, "I don't drop character 'til I've done the DVD commentary"?

a) Ben Stiller
b) Tom Cruise
c) Jack Black
d) Robert Downey, Jr.

2. The only color in the otherwise black and white *Schindler's List* is a red-hued:

a) rose
b) coat
c) bloodstain
d) ribbon

3. *Full Metal Jacket*'s bumbling recruit was nicknamed for what equally vapid TV character?

a) Homer Simpson
b) Gomer Pyle
c) Potsie Weber
d) Gilligan

4. *The Times* of London ranked what war movie the second-most historically inaccurate film?

a) *Das Boot*
b) *Gallipoli*
c) *Braveheart*
d) *Patton*

5. Which battle-hardened miniseries had 500 speaking parts and required 2,000 extras?

a) *Band of Brothers*
b) *Hatfields & McCoys*
c) *Joan of Arc*
d) *War and Remembrance*

1. Robert Downey, Jr.

He extended the joke, staying in character for the DVD commentary. Downey scored a surprise Oscar nominaton for the role.

2. coat

Following the film's release, a Krakow Ghetto survivor – coincidentally known for her red coat – wrote a memoir about her childhood experiences.

3. Gomer Pyle

Vincent D'Onofrio put on 70 pounds to play "Private Pyle," beating De Niro's Raging Bull record weight gain of 60 pounds.

4. *Braveheart*

Also listed: Mel Gibson's *The Patriot*. *The Times* asserted Gibson's character in real life was most likely a slave-owning, serial rapist.

5. *Band of Brothers*

Some days of filming required up to 14,000 rounds of ammunition. More pyrotechnics were used in the first 3 episodes than the entire *Saving Private Ryan* movie.

1. What is the profession of Jimmy Stewart's character in *Rear Window*?

a) thief
b) writer
c) photographer
d) he's unemployed

2. Which man behind *Buffy the Vampire Slayer* and *Firefly* helmed *The Avengers*?

a) J.J. Abrams
b) Joss Whedon
c) Jon Favreau
d) Michael Bay

3. Heath Ledger's Joker was informed by Sid Vicious and what other film villain?

a) Hannibal Lecter
b) Travis Bickle
c) Norman Bates
d) Alex De Large

4. Which action movie was *Empire* magazine's unlikely choice for the greatest Christmas film of all time?

a) *Rocky IV*
b) *Stalag 17*
c) *Die Hard*
d) *Lethal Weapon*

5. What is the only thing that Indiana Jones fears?

a) rats
b) snakes
c) spiders
d) needles

1. photographer

The film's love story was allegedly based on the affair between war photographer Robert Capa and actress Ingrid Bergman.

2. Joss Whedon

The Avengers is the third all-time highest grossing film, with over $1.5 billion. Only *Avatar* and *Titanic* earned more.

3. Alex De Large

The Clockwork Orange psycho informed many of Ledger's mannerisms. Ledger died just before the release – making the Joker his final role.

4. *Die Hard*

The film's head terrorist Hans is named after the real-life Austrian organist, Franz Gruber, who wrote and composed "Silent Night" in 1816.

5. snakes

The sound of thousands of slithering snakes was achieved by sticking fingers into cheese casserole and sliding wet sponges over skateboard rubber.

Biography
Questions

1. Which Oscar winner won praise for directing Emile Hirsch in *Into the Wild*?

a) Robert Redford
b) Ben Affleck
c) Sean Penn
d) Steven Soderbergh

2. The first Oscar win for playing an actual movie star was by *Ed Wood*'s Martin Landau who costarred as:

a) Orson Welles
b) Ed Wood
c) Bela Lugosi
d) Charlie Chaplin

3. *Cleopatra* effectively ended Elizabeth Taylor's marriage to which husband?

a) Eddie Fisher
b) Mike Todd
c) Richard Burton
d) Michael Wilding

4. *Inherit the Wind* chronicled a 1920's trial regarding what?

a) gangsters and Prohibition
b) racial integration
c) the Lindbergh kidnapping
d) teaching evolution in schools

5. Which British monarch was the stammering subject of *The King's Speech*?

a) Edward VIII
b) Albert IV
c) George V
d) George VI

Biography

1. Sean Penn

Zach Galifianakis improvised all of his lines because his character didn't have any scripted dialogue.

2. Bela Lugosi

Cate Blanchett is the only other star to accomplish the same feat with her role as Katharine Hepburn in the 2004 film *The Aviator*.

3. Eddie Fisher

The Vatican declared her affair with costar Richard Burton an act of "erotic vagrancy." They were married and divorced twice.

4. teaching evolution in schools

Based on the Scopes Monkey Trial, Dick York (*Bewitched*'s first Darrin) played the role modeled after teacher John Scopes.

5. George VI

Queen Elizabeth II, whose father was the title king (she was also depicted in it), was deeply touched by the film.

1. What did *Cheers'* Diane Chambers do professionally after she left Boston?

a) she became a psychiatrist
b) she became a housewife
c) she became a TV writer
d) she became a professor

2. What was *Mrs. Doubtfire's* first name?

a) Evangelina
b) Eleanora
c) Evelynanna
d) Euphegenia

3. When *The Producers* tried to stage a flop, they pick this offensive subject for the show:

a) slavery
b) AIDs
c) Adolf Hitler
d) the Indian Wars

4. What job does Dustin Hoffman's Dorothy Michaels take in *Tootsie*?

a) acting on a soap opera
b) secretary
c) business executive
d) fashion designer

5. Which star of an eponymous sitcom turned down the lead role on *Married...with Children*?

a) Ellen DeGeneres
b) Tracey Ullman
c) Roseanne Barr
d) Reba McEntire

Comedy

Answers

1. she became a TV writer

The series was initially intended to be set in Barstow, CA and was almost canceled after its first season. Luckily, the NBC president saw its potential.

2. Euphegenia

Robin Williams first performed the title character at Carnegie Hall during an Andy Kaufman show. He was pretending to be Kaufman's grandmother.

3. Adolf Hitler

Max and Leo plan to flee with their theater profits to Rio de Janeiro; ironically, the same place where many Nazis hid after WWII.

4. acting on a soap opera

He takes the TV role to raise money for a play entitled *Return to Love Canal* – named for the toxic waste disaster.

5. Roseanne Barr

Before Katey Sagal became Peg Bundy, it was offered to Roseanne, who turned it down and later gained fame on her own show.

1. Which *Sopranos* character was portrayed by the E Street Band's "Little Steven"?

   a) Christopher Moltisanti
   b) Sal Bonpensiero
   c) Silvio Dante
   d) Paulie Gualtieri

2. Italian-American actors De Niro and Pacino finally shared the screen in which crime film?

   a) *Casino*
   b) *Heat*
   c) *Goodfellas*
   d) *The Godfather Part II*

3. Julian Fellowes' *Downton Abbey* is akin to which film he scripted with the same themes?

   a) *Gosford Park*
   b) *The Young Victoria*
   C *The Queen*
   d) *Elizabeth*

4. *The Shawshank Redemption* is based on a novella that named which siren in its title?

   a) Lana Turner
   b) Marilyn Monroe
   c) Jayne Mansfield
   d) Rita Hayworth

5. In which HBO show did flame-haired Claire put a human foot in the locker of a former beau?

   a) *Big Love*
   b) *Six Feet Under*
   c) *Deadwood*
   d) *The Sopranos*

1. **Silvio Dante**

   A longtime member of Springsteen's Jersey-born band, Van Zandt contributed many of the lead guitar licks to *Born to Run*.

2. *Heat*

   Both were in *Godfather Part II* but never in the same scene. It was another 21 years before they were united onscreen.

3. *Gosford Park*

   The show has used some of the same sets that the film used a decade earlier; Maggie Smith starred in both productions.

4. **Rita Hayworth**

   Stephen King's story was titled *Rita Hayworth and Shawshank Redemption*. In it, Red gets Andy a poster of the film icon.

5. *Six Feet Under*

   She was the hearse-driving third child of the Fishers, who ran a funeral home, giving her easy access to stray feet.

1. Whose computer system did Matthew Broderick hack into in the 1980's hit, *WarGames*?

a) FBI
b) NORAD
c) his school
d) a major bank

2. What is the name of Bart's teacher on *The Simpsons*?

a) Helen Lovejoy
b) Agnes Skinner
c) Edna Krabappel
d) Maude Flanders

3. What game show asked kid-testants to answer questions or do a messy physical challenge?

a) *Wild & Crazy Kids*
b) *Double Dare*
c) *Global Guts*
d) *Legends of the Hidden Temple*

4. Whose pirate's treasure were *The Goonies* hunting for in Astoria?

a) One-Eyed Willie
b) Blackbeard
c) Captain Kidd
d) Benito Bonito

5. Who played the title teacher on the junior high version of *Saved By the Bell*?

a) Sally Field
b) Diane Keaton
c) Patty Duke
d) Hayley Mills

1. NORAD

The film's NORAD command center was the most costly set ever built as of 1983; it turned out to be more elaborate than the real thing.

2. Edna Krabappel

Actress Tilda Swinton modeled her *Burn After Reading* character's hairstyle on Mrs. Krabappel's.

3. *Double Dare*

In a strange coincidence, host Marc Summers had O.C.D., and compulsively cleaned in his everyday life.

4. One-Eyed Willie

The cast wasn't allowed to see the 105-ft. pirate ship until the final scenes were shot. The ship was later offered for free to anyone who wanted it.

5. Hayley Mills

The *Good Morning, Miss Bliss* star is best-remembered for her roles in *The Parent Trap*, *That Darn Cat!* and *Pollyanna*.

1. Filming *The Birds'* one-minute final attack scene took a week and put who in the hospital?

  a) Alfred Hitchcock
  b) Tippi Hedren
  c) Jessica Tandy
  d) Veronica Cartwright

2. In what month and year was *Rosemary's Baby* born?

  a) July, 1964
  b) June, 1966
  c) August, 1968
  d) December, 1969

3. The cast and crew of which 1970's horror classic were famously plagued by bad "luck"?

  a) *Jaws*
  b) *The Omen*
  c) *Night of the Living Dead*
  d) *Halloween*

4. For which classic horror character was *Carrie*'s high school named?

  a) Norman Bates
  b) Regan MacNeil
  c) Jack Torrance
  d) Rosemary Woodhouse

5. An early cut of *Frankenstein* gave the monster what name, fitting for a created being?

  a) Christopher
  b) John
  c) Sonny
  d) Adam

1. Tippi Hedren

Hitchcock had live birds hurled at his star and many were tied to her clothing. She broke down after one clawed her eye.

2. June, 1966

He was born in 6/66. The movie was shot in Manhattan's famed Dakota Building, where John Lennon lived.

3. *The Omen*

Separate planes carrying the star and producer were hit by lightning. On day 1 of the shoot several principal crew members got into a head-on car crash.

4. Norman Bates

The Exorcist's Linda Blair auditioned to play *Carrie*, as did Melanie Griffith, daughter of *The Birds* star Tippi Hedren.

5. Adam

The declaration at his "birth" – "It's alive! It's alive!" – was ranked among the AFI's top movie quotes.

1. Who was the very first host of *The Tonight Show*?

   a) Ernie Kovacs
   b) Johnny Carson
   c) Jack Paar
   d) Steve Allen

2. After being termed the "Dick Clark of Generation-Y" on TRL, Carson Daly started hosting:

   a) *Last Call*
   b) *The Late Late Show*
   c) *Late Night*
   d) *The Midnight Hour*

3. How many co-hosts did Regis have on his N.Y.-based morning show before retiring in 2011?

   a) two co-hosts
   b) three co-hosts
   c) four co-hosts
   d) five co-hosts

4. What cable show did Jimmy Kimmel host prior to getting his late-night gig on ABC?

   a) *The Man Show*
   b) *The Daily Show*
   c) *Total Request Live*
   d) *Comedy Central Presents*

5. *Big Brother* host Julie Chen began co-hosting which daytime show in 2010?

   a) *The View*
   b) *The Talk*
   c) *The Chew*
   d) *The Early Show*

1. Steve Allen

When it debuted in '54 he predicted "this show is going to go on forever." Paar, Carson, Leno and O'Brien succeeded him.

2. *Last Call*

He got NBC's middle-of-the-night slot after Conan's Late Night in 2003, where, as of 2012, he's had almost 1,000 shows.

3. four co-hosts

Cyndy Garvey, wife of baseball star Steve Garvey, was the first co-host in 1983. Kathie Lee (co-host #3) joined in 1985.

4. *The Man Show*

While hosting *The Man Show*, he also hosted *Win Ben Stein's Money*. He cites David Letterman as his role model.

5. *The Talk*

Chen, whose shows air on CBS, is married to network president Les Moonves. Her *Talk* co-hosts include Sharon Osbourne.

1. Where did Carrie and Mr. Big finally say "I do" in *Sex and the City*?

   a) the NY Public Library
   b) a community garden
   c) in a small Manhattan chapel
   d) city hall

2. What show beget the theory that TV shows are ruined if two lead characters become an off-screen couple?

   a) *Cheers*
   b) *The X-Files*
   c) *Moonlighting*
   d) *Remington Steele*

3. Where did childhood sweethearts Kevin and Winnie have their first kiss?

   a) in a barn
   b) at a Fourth of July picnic
   c) at the movies
   d) in the woods

4. For what publication was Robert Kincaid on assignment in *Bridges of Madison County*?

   a) *Life*
   b) *Architectural Digest*
   c) *National Geographic*
   d) *Traveler*

5. Which heralded American poet's work was part of Annie's staged seduction in *Bull Durham*?

   a) Robert Frost
   b) Walt Whitman
   c) E. E. Cummings
   d) Emily Dickinson

1. city hall

The famous tutu Parker struts in the opening credits was only $5 in a vintage store. Naturally blonde-haired Cynthia Nixon had to dye her hair red for the role of Miranda.

2. *Moonlighting*

Bruce Willis and Cybill Shepherd's epic chemistry fizzled out after they got together, forever striking fear in the hearts of showrunners.

3. in the woods

The couple briefly stopped being friends on the show because Danica McKellar had a growth spurt and looked awkward with Fred Savage.

4. *National Geographic*

Clint Eastwood's search for younger actresses to play the lead was fruitless, so he took his mother's advice and hired Meryl Streep.

5. Walt Whitman

With Nuke tied to her bed, she recites lines from Whitman's "I Sing the Body Electric" from *Leaves of Grass*.

1. Which future Oscar winner played opposite David Bowie in *Labyrinth*?

a) Jennifer Connelly
b) Helen Hunt
c) Kate Winslet
d) Natalie Portman

2. What film's CGI effects convinced James Cameron that he could make *Avatar* as he envisioned it?

a) *Rise of the Planet of the Apes*
b) *Titanic*
c) *The Lord of the Rings*
d) *Shrek*

3. Which actor spent their early 20s going to Harvard and filming *Stars Wars* movies?

a) Carrie Fisher
b) Hayden Christensen
c) Mark Hamill
d) Natalie Portman

4. What movie did popular scientist Carl Sagan consider the best time travel film ever made?

a) *Time After Time*
b) *Back to the Future Part II*
c) *The Time Machine*
d) *Planet of the Apes*

5. What sci-fi TV show inspired screenwriter Chris Carter to create *The X-Files*?

a) *Alien Nation*
b) *V*
c) *The Outer Limits*
d) *Kolchak: The Night Stalker*

1. Jennifer Connelly

Another future Oscar winner, Marisa Tomei, also auditioned for the lead. This film was the final feature directed by Jim Henson.

2. *The Lord of the Rings*

Each frame of CGI animation (there are 24 frame in one second) took about 47 hours to digitally create.

3. Natalie Portman

Her character's double was played by a then-unknown Keira Knightley – they were identical when in full makeup.

4. *Back to the Future Part II*

Author of the sci-fi novel *Contact*, Sagan praised the movie for the accuracy in which it addressed multiple timelines.

5. *Kolchak: The Night Stalker*

While Kolchak was his primary influence, *The Twilight Zone*, *Night Gallery*, and other conspiracy movies also informed it.

1. Steven Spielberg's *Empire of the Sun* launched the career of what 12-year-old future Oscar winner?

a) Christian Bale
b) Heath Ledger
c) Daniel Day-Lewis
d) Sean Penn

2. Which *Saving Private Ryan* star was the only castmate **not** required to go to boot camp?

a) Tom Hanks
b) Edward Burns
c) Matt Damon
d) Tom Sizemore

3. What did censors suggest the stars of *From Here to Eternity* wear for the iconic beach scene?

a) Hawaiian shirts
b) pajamas
c) bathrobes
d) coats

4. African-American cowboy Bose Ikard inspired Danny Glover's character Deets in:

a) *Roots*
b) *Lonesome Dove*
c) *North and South*
d) *The Thorn Birds*

5. What Old West-set satire was among the American Film Institute's top ten comedies?

a) *City Slickers*
b) *Blazing Saddles*
c) *Back to the Future Part III*
d) *Cat Ballou*

War & Western

1. Christian Bale

The National Board of Review awarded him Best Ever Performance by a Juvenile – an award they created just for him.

2. Matt Damon

Spielberg let Damon skip exhausting army training in hopes it would foster genuine resentment between him and the other actors.

3. bathrobes

Myths about the film – like the Mob putting a horse head in someone's bed to get Sinatra a part – were later fictionalized in Coppola's *The Godfather*.

4. *Lonesome Dove*

The miniseries used sets from the feature film *Silverado*, which was also a western starring Danny Glover as a cowboy.

5. *Blazing Saddles*

Mel Brooks offered John Wayne a part but he declined saying, "I can't be in this picture, it's too dirty . . . but I'll be first in line to see it."

1. According to *Pulp Fiction* what do the French call the "Quarter Pounder with Cheese"?

   a) "Le Cheesy Mac"
   b) "Le Royale with Cheese"
   c) "Le Grande with Cheese"
   d) "Le Cheesy King"

2. Future 007, Pierce Brosnan, spent his teenage years performing what act in a circus?

   a) walking a tightrope
   b) lion taming
   c) fire eating
   d) acrobatics

3. Which costar's hilarious off-camera antics led Wolfgang Peterson to dub their movie *Air Force "Fun"*?

   a) Harrison Ford
   b) Glenn Close
   c) William H. Macy
   d) Gary Oldman

4. Which crime film posed the question: "Who is Keyser Söze?"

   a) *Se7en*
   b) *Pulp Fiction*
   c) *The Usual Suspects*
   d) *Chinatown*

5. Bill Paxton and Helen Hunt's characters reunited in *Twister* to launch a device named what?

   a) The POD
   b) DOROTHY
   c) The WASPS NEST
   d) TOTO

1. "Le Royale with Cheese"

In truth, the French call the burger a "McRoyal" and, if it's ordered with cheese, it's called "Royal Cheese."

2. fire eating

He learned the skill at 16 and performed on public streets. He was soon "discovered" by a circus agent who offered him a prime gig under the big top.

3. Gary Oldman

Peterson's request to see the real Air Force One was initially denied by the White House – one call from Harrison Ford changed their minds.

4. *The Usual Suspects*

Kevin Spacey, who plays Verbal Kint, won the Best Supporting Actor Oscar for what Rolling Stong called a "balls-out brilliant performance."

5. DOROTHY

Both actors were temporarily blinded by a special effects lamp on-set. Paxton described the injury as a sunburn on their eyeballs.

1. What protagonist traveled to London and stayed at Kingsley Hall, in real life and on film?

a) Itzhak Stern
b) Georges Méliès
c) Mohandas Gandhi
d) Elvis Presley

2. Robert Redford lived in a historic Washington, D.C. hotel while making what movie?

a) *Three Days of the Condor*
b) *All the President's Men*
c) *Quiz Show*
d) *The Conspirator*

3. *A Cry in the Dark* vilified what wild animal?

a) lion
b) hyena
c) dingo
d) shark

4. Who stopped by *SNL* to tell Jesse Eisenberg he found *The Social Network* "interesting"?

a) Justin Timberlake
b) Mark Zuckerberg
c) Steve Jobs
d) Brad Pitt

5. What biopic was stripped of references to Louis Farrakhan when he threatened its director?

a) *JFK*
b) *All the President's Men*
c) *J. Edgar*
d) *Malcolm X*

Biography
Answers

1. Mohandas Gandhi

Ben Kingsley so closely resembled
Mohandas K. Gandhi, many Indians
believed he was his ghost.

2. *All the President's Men*

Fittingly, he stayed in the Watergate. He and
Dustin Hoffman also sat in on *Washington
Post* news conferences to prepare.

3. dingo

In 2012, a new coroner's examination
conclusively ruled that a dingo did in fact
take Lindy Chamberlain's baby.

4. Mark Zuckerberg

All of the plaid shirts and fleece Eisenberg
wore in the film were identical to those of his
real-life counterpart.

5. *Malcolm X*

It was the first movie ever granted permission
to film in Mecca, however Spike Lee couldn't
go because he's not Muslim.

1. Who lived onscreen in Mayberry, Modesto, and Milwaukee before narrating the Bluths' saga?

a) Henry Winkler
b) Michael J. Fox
c) Ron Howard
d) Don Knotts

2. What landmark did the Griswolds back a car into and knock down on their European Vacation?

a) Stonehenge
b) Leaning Tower of Pisa
c) London's Tower Bridge
d) Eiffel Tower

3. Sixties sitcom star Marlo Thomas (*That Girl*) married which daytime talk show host?

a) Maury Povich
b) Dr. Phil
c) Phil Donahue
d) Jerry Springer

4. Which show was the most prolific Emmy-winning sitcom of the 1970s?

a) *All in the Family*
b) *The Mary Tyler Moore Show*
c) *M*A*S*H*
d) *The Odd Couple*

5. Which sitcom ended with a legendary twist that revealed the whole show had been a dream?

a) *M*A*S*H*
b) *Newhart*
c) *Mork & Mindy*
d) *Doogie Howser, M.D.*

1. Ron Howard

He was *Andy Griffith*'s Opie, a lead in George Lucas' *American Graffiti*, and *Happy Days*' Richie. Three decades later he narrated *Arrested Development*.

2. Stonehenge

Juliette Lewis, Johnny Galecki and Anthony Michael Hall all played Griswold kids, and were recast in each film.

3. Phil Donahue

Three decades after her hit show, Thomas guest-starred on *Friends*, playing the mother of 1990s "It Girl" Jennifer Aniston.

4. *The Mary Tyler Moore Show*

Though *M*A*S*H* is one of the most beloved shows ever, it only won a third as many trophies as Mary Tyler Moore.

5. *Newhart*

At the end of Bob Newhart' second sitcom he woke-up next to Suzanne Pleschette, who played his wife in his first show.

1) *One Flew Over the Cuckoo's Nest* introduced filmgoers to which literary villain?

a) Nurse Ratched
b) Alex Forrest
c) Hannibal Lecter
d) Alex De Large

2) Which laid-back cinema star proved his mettle as a serious actor in *A Time to Kill*?

a) Keanu Reeves
b) Sean Penn
c) Matthew McConaughey
d) James Franco

3) What Best Picture was originally about Amy Fisher before the draft evolved into fiction?

a) *The Departed*
b) *American Beauty*
c) *Million Dollar Baby*
d) *Crash*

4) Which gangster movie unintentionally became the most seminal film in hip-hop culture?

a) *Scarface*
b) *The Godfather*
c) *Goodfellas*
d) *Pulp Fiction*

5) Which famed *Death of a Salesman* playwright wrote the first draft of *On the Waterfront*?

a) Edward Albee
b) Eugene O'Neill
c) Arthur Miller
d) Thornton Wilder

1. Nurse Ratched

The despicable nurse who berated and tormented psychiatric patients was ranked #5 on the American Film Institute's list of top villains.

2. Matthew McConaughey

Often identified with his *Dazed and Confused* role, he's a lawyer on a mission in the John Grisham big-screen adaptation.

3. *American Beauty*

Allusions to *Lolita* recurred in the film; Amy Fisher was nicknamed in the media as "the Long Island Lolita."

4. *Scarface*

The De Palma movie, about a Cuban refugee who ascends to power as a drug lord, is a common favorite among rappers.

5. Arthur Miller

Miller was replaced with a new writer after he criticized the director, Kazan, for naming Communists in the film industry.

1. What kind of accent did Mike Myers give *Shrek*?

a) English
b) Irish
c) Scottish
d) Australian

2. What food manufacturer originally financed *Willy Wonka & the Chocolate Factory*?

a) Coca-Cola
b) Hershey's
c) Quaker Oats Company
d) Wonder Bread

3. What did a young boy wish on before being transformed into an adult Tom Hanks in *Big*?

a) a genie carnival machine
b) a shooting star
c) birthday candles
d) a witch's potion

4. What kind of dog was *Beethoven*?

a) Siberian Husky
b) Golden Retriever
c) St. Bernard
d) Bernese Mountain Dog

5. What was the name of the old gangster movie the McCallister family watch in *Home Alone*?

a) *Keep the Change*
b) *Filthy Animals*
c) *Tommy-Gun Justice*
d) *Angels with Filthy Souls*

1. Scottish

Eddie Murphy was nominated for a
BAFTA Award for voicing Donkey –
the first mainstream acting award nod
for a voiceover.

2. Quaker Oats Company

The combination to the primary door of the
chocolate factory is "99-44-100% pure,"
which was borrowed from an Ivory Soap ad.

3. a genie carnival machine

Director Penny Marshall had Tom Hanks'
younger version act out each grown-up scene
first, then had Hanks copy his mannerisms.

4. St. Bernard

Before Dean Jones played *Beethoven*'s evil
vet, he was an animal lover in Disney's *That
Darn Cat!* and *The Ugly Dachshund*.

5. *Angels with Filthy Souls*

Joe Pesci had to do many retakes because
he'd swear reflexively when he got hit.
Director Chris Columbus instructed him to
yell "fridge" instead.

1. Despite his infamous *War of the Worlds* radio broadcast, who refused to be involved in the film?

a) Orson Welles
b) Walter Winchell
c) H. G. Wells
d) Alfred Hitchcock

2. Which *Interview with the Vampire* actor's casting initially upset Anne Rice?

a) Brad Pitt
b) Antonio Banderas
c) Christian Slater
d) Tom Cruise

3. What was used to simulate blood in horror classic *Night of the Living Dead*?

a) chocolate syrup
b) corn syrup dyed red
c) ketchup
d) red paint

4. In what U.S. state do *True Blood*'s vampires and other beings wreak havoc and look for equality?

a) Georgia
b) South Carolina
c) Louisiana
d) Tennessee

5. Hollywood's *Dracula* was played by what actor who shared the real Count's home country?

a) Boris Karloff
b) Lon Chaney
c) Bela Lugosi
d) Rudolph Valentino

1. Orson Welles

His Halloween 1938 radio broadcast led to pandemonium. It took years for a film version to come to fruition (1953).

2. Tom Cruise

After seeing the movie her opinion changed. During filming, he often stood on a box to make up for his lack of height.

3. chocolate syrup

Though it was made in 1968, the film was in black and white, so dark brown chocolate syrup looked appropriate on-screen.

4. Louisiana

It's set in Bon Temps, named after the iconic Cajun saying, "Laissez les bon temps rouler!" or "Let the good times roll!"

5. Bela Lugosi

When the Romanian actor died in 1956, he was buried in the black cape that he wore in his *Dracula* movies.

1. The first Bernard Pivot-inspired question James Lipton asks *Actors Studio* guests is about their:

a) favorite sound
b) favorite word
c) Favorite movie
d) favorite curse word

2. Who is considered the pioneer of the daytime talk show format?

a) Oprah Winfrey
b) Geraldo Rivera
c) Dick Clark
d) Phil Donahue

3. Oprah was taken to court after she was accused of defaming what industry on her show?

a) poultry industry
b) beef industry
c) dairy industry
d) processed "junk" food industry

4. Dr. Oz is a real physician and one of the nation's leading specialists in what field?

a) cardiothoracic surgery
b) vascular surgery
c) orthopedic surgery
d) neurosurgery

5. On whose couch did Tom Cruise jump in 2005 as he proclaimed his love for Katie Holmes?

a) Ellen DeGeneres
b) Jay Leno
c) Oprah Winfrey
d) David Letterman

Reality TV & Talk Show

Answers

1. favorite word

Only six actors have visited Lipton's master class twice: Tom Hanks, Alec Baldwin, Billy Crystal, Anthony Hopkins, Sarah Jessica Parker and Mike Myers.

2. Phil Donahue

While hosting a late '50s daytime show in Dayton he interviewed Martin Luther King Jr., Malcolm X and Jimmy Hoffa.

3. beef industry

Her 1996 interview with Michael Jackson was then the fourth-highest rated program in TV history and most watched interview.

4. cardiothoracic surgery

At University of Pennsylvania School of Medicine, Oz earned an MD and MBA, while holding down position of class president.

5. Oprah Winfrey

It made "jumping the couch" a synonym for "going overboard." *Entertainment Weekly* said: "Lesson learned: Tell, don't show."

1. *Titanic* was the top-grossing film all time until it was surpassed by what movie?

a) *The Avengers*
b) *The Hunger Games*
c) *Avatar*
d) *The Deathly Hallows Part II*

2. In 1925 Samuel Goldwyn asked what doctor to write a screenplay about Antony and Cleopatra?

a) Margaret Mead
b) Ivan Pavlov
c) Louis Leakey
d) Sigmund Freud

3. Barbra Streisand scored her first number-one single with the theme from which film?

a) *Hello, Dolly!*
b) *What's Up, Doc?*
c) *A Star Is Born*
d) *The Way We Were*

4. What incendiary film caused "well-dressed wives" to vomit, according to *The Village Voice*?

a) *Last Tango in Paris*
b) *Bonnie and Clyde*
c) *Bob & Carol & Ted & Alice*
d) *Lolita*

5. Who directed a modernized adaptation of the Bard that made Leonardo DiCaprio a heartthrob?

a) James Cameron
b) Baz Luhrmann
c) Kenneth Branagh
d) John Madden

1. *Avatar*

   James Cameron made both top-earning films; he spent 15 years working on *Titanic*, even after it was initially released.

2. **Sigmund Freud**

   Freud's psychoanalysis was all the rage in the '20s, prompting the studio boss to offer him $100,000 for a screenplay.

3. *The Way We Were*

   The title track won an Academy Award for Best Song. The star was also nominated for Best Actress.

4. *Last Tango in Paris*

   It's one of the few mainstream movies from the 1960s-'80s to receive the MPAA's X-rating, along with *Midnight Cowboy* and *A Clockwork Orange*.

5. **Baz Luhrmann**

   In addition to *Romeo + Juliet*, Luhrmann also made the musical romantic dramedy *Moulin Rouge!* and helmed a retelling of *The Great Gatsby* in 2012.

1. Who was not among the historical figures detained during *Bill & Ted's Excellent Adventure*?

a) George Washington
b) Napoleon
c) Joan of Arc
d) Billy the Kid

2. Which John Hughes-penned character was described as "Mary Poppins with breasts"?

a) *Splash*'s Madison
b) *Miracle on 34th Street*'s Dorey
c) *Weird Science*'s Lisa
d) *The Princess Bride*'s Buttercup

3. What physically expressive actor provided the articulation of Gollum in *Lord of the Rings*?

a) Robin Williams
b) Andy Serkis
c) Toby Jones
d) Michael Sheen

4. What is the name of the self-aware computer in *2001: A Space Odyssey*?

a) KITT
b) Skynet
c) Colossus
d) HAL 9000

5. When did the Borg phrase "Resistance is futile" enter the *Star Trek* lexicon?

a) *Star Trek*
b) *Star Trek: The Next Generation*
c) *Star Trek: First Contact*
d) *Star Trek: Voyager*

1. George Washington

The film's infamous time-machine phone booth was given away in a Nintendo Power contest to promote the Bill & Ted video game.

2. *Weird Science*'s Lisa

Hughes wrote the *Weird Science* script in two days. Robert Downey, Jr. played a bully in one of his first feature roles.

3. Andy Serkis

Serkis has become well-known for his CGI live-animation work. He also played Caesar in *Rise of the Planet of the Apes*.

4. HAL 9000

Director Kubrick wanted insurance in case intelligent alien life was found before the film's release, but he was denied.

5. *Star Trek: The Next Generation*

The warnings generally begin with "We are the Borg" before demanding something and ending with the tagline.

1. The cowboy crew in *The Wild Bunch* took its name from the gang of what real Old West outlaw?

   a) Jesse James
   b) Butch Cassidy
   c) Billy the Kid
   d) Doc Holliday

2. Which western movie was an allegory about Joseph McCarthy's Communist witch hunts?

   a) *True Grit*
   b) *Blazing Saddles*
   c) *High Noon*
   d) *The Treasure of the Sierra Madre*

3. What Clint Eastwood film is one of only three westerns to have won Oscar's Best Picture?

   a) *The Outlaw Josey Wales*
   b) *Unforgiven*
   c) *The Good, the Bad and the Ugly*
   d) *A Fistful of Dollars*

4. In the Old West classic *The Searchers*, John Wayne played a veteran of what war?

   a) Civil War
   b) World War I
   c) Mexican-American War
   d) Spanish-American War

5. *Triumph of the Will* was a political propaganda associated with what country?

   a) United States
   b) Soviet Union
   c) Germany
   d) Great Britain

1. Butch Cassidy

They were also known as the "Hole in the Wall Gang." John Wayne criticized the film, saying *The Wild Bunch* destroyed the myth of the Old West.

2. *High Noon*

Specifically, it was about Hollywood's failure to stand up for indicted artists. It's President Bill Clinton's favorite film.

3. *Unforgiven*

The critically-acclaimed film, which was expected to be Eastwood's final picture in which he both directed and acted, won 4 Oscars, including Best Picture.

4. Civil War

Natalie Wood was still in high school during the making of the film. To her classmates' delight, she was often picked up by John Wayne himself.

5. Germany

While Leni Riefenstahl claimed it was just a documentary, the film glorified Nazis and listed Hitler as an unofficial producer.